Pelee Portrait
Canada's Southern Treasures

Pelee Portrait
Canada's Southern Treasures

Published by DT Publishing Group, Inc.

in association with

Point Pelee National Park | The Friends of Point Pelee

and

Pelee Island Heritage Centre

AND MADE POSSIBLE THROUGH THE GENEROUS SUPPORT OF THE FOLLOWING SPONSORS:

PRIMARY SPONSORSHIP
Pelee Island Winery

SECONDARY SPONSORSHIP
Family Tradition Foods Inc.

FRIENDS SPONSORSHIP
Century 21 Erie Shores Realty Inc.
Corporation of the Municipality of Leamington, Economic Development Office
Essex Community Futures Development Corporation/Société d'aide au développement des collectivités
Owen Sound Transportation
Sun-Brite Canning Ltd.

PATRON SPONSORSHIP
Comfort Inn Leamington
Gulliver Insurance Brokers Ltd.
Mennonite Savings & Credit Union
Woodslee Credit Union
www.pelee.com

DT Publishing Group gratefully recognizes the staff of Point Pelee National Park of Canada for provision of images, access to library resources and content review.
Special thanks to Ron Tiessen, Curator of the Pelee Island Heritage Centre and Lea Martell, General Manager of the Friends of Point Pelee
for their contributions to the content of this publication.

Pelee Portrait
Canada's Southern Treasures

Copyright © 2002
by DT Publishing Group, Inc.

DT Publishing Group, Inc.
2276 Rosedene Rd.
St. Ann's, ON LoR 1Yo
Tel: (905) 957-6016; Fax: (905) 957-6017

Canadian Cataloguing in Publication Data

Pelee Portrait - Canada's Southern Treasures
ISBN 0-9686013-1-6
Printed and Bound in Canada

SPECIAL SALES
Pelee Portrait - Canada's Southern Treasures, is available at special discounts for bulk purchases for sales promotions or premiums. For more information, contact DT Publishing Group, Inc.

PUBLISHER & EXECUTIVE EDITOR
Jeffrey Tiessen

CONTRIBUTING EDITORS
Kimberly Tiessen
Ron Tiessen

CONTRIBUTING PHOTOGRAPHERS
Jim Flynn
Ethan Meleg
Rob Tymstra

ART DIRECTION & DESIGN
Norm Lourenco R.G.D.

SPONSORSHIP SALES
Jeffrey Yamaguchi

RESEARCH ASSISTANTS
Mary Ellen Havlik
Brenda McCarthy
Hilda Tiessen

contents

1

publisher's message

We were the boys and girls of summer.

Our playing field was framed by the peerless diversity of Canada's Sunparlour… Leamington, Kingsville, Wheatley and all the villages and hamlets in between that we called home. We toiled in their fields and greenhouses and frolicked on their beaches. We explored in their woodlots, fished their waters and camped in their parks. We worked and played on Canada's southernmost soils and in its warmest waters.

This was southwestern Ontario – the Pelee region – Canada's geographical peculiarity. Surrounded by water on three sides (four sides on Pelee Island), the United States was our friendly neighbour to the north, as well as to the south. Many of our influences were culturally American, including our migrant summer friends who answered the call of the local cottage industry. At the same time, we took great childhood pride in those things about us that were distinctly Canadian… hockey's Maple Leafs and Canadiens… the Canada Goose… Canada Dry.

We were kids.

Sometimes we could not see Pelee's forest for the trees. Many a school excursion took us to nearby Point Pelee National Park, but the magnificence of the brilliantly tinted songbirds and delicately patterned butterflies too often escaped our appreciation. Lake Erie's wealth of catch seemed nothing more than a fishing given. For us, the rare and unique Carolinian forest that canopied our neighbourhoods was cherished more for its sanctuary from the heat and humidity of a Pelee summer, and for its treehouse potential of course, than for its extraordinary array of species.

But Pelee leaves an indelible impression, even on its heedless youth. Our memories of those endless days of summer have matured into a sealed bundle of singular childhood recollections… Trillium spotting at Scout camp at Point Pelee… Largemouth Bass fishing off the rocky shores of Pelee Island… the sweet smell of the tomato harvest wafting from the local canneries.

And in the fall, the collective urgency of the fluttery Monarchs. In the winter, ice skating on the Park's frozen marsh. In the spring, the month-long vigil for the Red-winged Blackbird, arguably Pelee's first sign of the ensuing season. And always, the cropped silhouette of Pelee Island on the south horizon, a fixture of balance in a fickle lake.

It is this medley of images that seeded the designs for *Pelee Portrait - Canada's Southern Treasures*. A grown-up passion for natural history and human heritage germinated its production. Point Pelee National Park is a jewel of nature: small, rare and valuable. One of the most-visited Parks in Canada, and among the most renowned in North America, it shares with Pelee and Middle Islands the distinction of a natural habitat unique to the rest of Canada. Man's involvement historically at Point Pelee is second to none among Canada's other National Parks. And on and around Pelee Island and Middle Island, the colourful tales and traditions of human occupation inspire the imagination and stir the sense of adventure.

It is in this spirit of natural beauty and storied human history that *Pelee Portrait* is presented. It is intended to stand as a celebration of the hidden gems that we call Point Pelee, Pelee Island and Middle Island. It is meant to share all that makes this tiny yet hugely diverse oasis one of Canada's greatest treasures.

And finally, it is a compelling compilation of photography and rich narrative from a passionate gang of boys and girls of Pelee summers past.

Jeffrey A. Tiessen
Publisher

Tiessen, age 5, at Point Pelee National Park; (1970).

contributors

Norm Lourenco R.G.D.
Toronto, Ontario

A native of Leamington, Norm Lourenco grew up with Point Pelee as his playground. He could often be found at the Point fishing, canoeing or hiking in the summer and skating with friends on the marsh in winter. Point Pelee and Pelee Island were often the subjects of Lourenco's art assignments in high school and later in college. Now a practicing Graphic Designer, working in Toronto, Lourenco was very excited to once again have the Pelee region as the subject of an assignment.

Kimberly Tiessen
Toronto, Ontario

Born and raised in Leamington, Kimberly Tiessen spent most of her summers on Pelee Island. Much of her time was spent hosting at Mill Point Lodge (now the Tin Goose) – the one-time family owned and operated bed & breakfast. She also worked in the historical Pelee Club's great dining hall, and as a summer camp counsellor for the Island's youth. Tiessen's employment in Leamington and Kingsville kept her immersed in the tourism industry as a visitor information officer and a Pelee Island Winery tour host respectively. She also worked in information services at Point Pelee National Park.

A Seneca College Journalism graduate now living in Toronto, Tiessen is an award-winning television producer, an extensively published freelance writer and a respected book editor, but makes time each summer and fall to return to her family's Island cottage at Vin Villa Estates.

Ethan Meleg
Tobermory, Ontario

Ethan Meleg grew up in the Pelee area and spent many seasons on Pelee Island working as a naturalist. The rich diversity of the Island catalyzed his passion for nature photography. Meleg now works as a professional naturalist and photographer, with his photo work published throughout North America. He is the primary author of *A Guide to Exploring Pelee Island Wildlife*. Now a resident of Ontario's Bruce Peninsula, Meleg spends much of his time exploring the natural world with his camera, whether on distant travels or in his backyard. Visit his website to see more of Ethan Meleg's compelling images: www.ethanmeleg.com.

Rob Tymstra
Sarnia, Ontario

Rob Tymstra has been a nature photographer and writer for over 25 years. He is widely published in textbooks, calendars, magazines and scientific journals. Presently, he spends most of his camera time behind a movie lens, shooting feature films.

Tymstra is an avid birder and has travelled to more than 50 countries in search of birds to be added to his sightings list. He is a Fellow of the Explorers Club and an Associate Member of the Canadian Society of Cinematographers. The Erie Islands rank highly among his favourite places on the planet. To contact Rob Tymstra, email: birdman@ebtech.net.

Ron Tiessen
Pelee Island, Ontario

Raised in the Leamington area, Ron Tiessen chose to live on Pelee Island in 1979. He has been Curator of the Pelee Island Heritage Centre since its inception. Author of a number of books pertaining to the Island's story, his curiosity about his neighbourhood has not yet waned.

Kimberly Tiessen

Norm Lourenco R.G.D.

Ethan Meleg

Ron Tiessen

Rob Tymstra

Point Pelee National Park

Canada is a land patterned in vistas of mountain and plains, tundra and forest, coastline and Great Lakes shore. It is a country rich in natural and cultural heritage, where landscape has shaped the destiny of its people. Thus, the role played by Provincial and National Parks in Canadian society is an important one. And it is complex. Today's Parks must accommodate both man and nature, and yet retain their natural integrity. Parks are sources of knowledge of natural living communities: knowledge that is essential to our understanding of how we relate to our world. At the same time, parklands are a tonic to modern man; there is sanctuary and sensory adventure in a natural setting.

Types of parks vary from those with fountains and manicured lawns, to near arctic wilderness preserves. Towns and cities often maintain a green-space of shaded park benches. Playgrounds and ball diamonds are not uncommon in the suburbs. Provincial governments support a variety of parks, from roadside promenades and campgrounds, to limited access wilderness areas.

Canada's federal government, in Parks Canada, also administers a diverse park system which includes Historic Canals and Waterways, Historic Sites, National Marine Parks and National Parks. There are 145 National Historic Sites in Canada, from Louisbourg in Nova Scotia to the Klondike in the Yukon. The 39 National Parks, an expanding part of the system, preserve valuable natural landscapes and human heritage across the face of Canada, for all Canadians, for all time.

Most Canadians today are city dwellers. Parks Canada ensures the existence of outlets and satisfaction for the needs of many who need to escape the city. National Parks are quiet places – sanctums for endless opportunity of learning about

While the Windsor to Toronto corridor represents only one-quarter of one percent of Canada's land mass, 25 percent of the Canadian population lives there, all within 360 kilometres (220 miles) of Point Pelee National Park.

nature and restoring peace of mind. There are opportunities for those who wish a scenic drive, a solitary paddle, a boating trip or an eventful hike. Canada's National Parks recognize and serve man's recreational needs, asking only that its visitors respect the land and its past in return.

In the southernmost part of Ontario lies the cusp-shaped Point Pelee foreland that extends 16 kilometres (10 miles) into Lake Erie. Its base is some six kilometres extending from Leamington's Seacliffe Park to the mouth of Hillman Creek. The breadth of the northern boundary of Point Pelee National Park is only four kilometres, gradually narrowing to form an ever-shifting sharp tip. Point Pelee is a unique combination of landform and life. It is an unusual sandspit formation, which due to United States-Canada boundary positioning is the most southern ground in mainland Canada. Shallow Lake Erie almost surrounds the Park, and the climate, moderated by the lake, suits many southern forms of plants and animals. Lake Erie is forever changing water levels and soil conditions in the marsh. The entire sandspit is young, less than 10,000 years of age and continues to develop even today in the evolving lake. Point Pelee reflects the restless moods of the lake by its shifting shorelines, and in its unsettled living community.

The area of the Park is nearly 16 square kilometres. Despite its diminutive proportions (compared to other national parks), Point Pelee National Park is fantastically varied in character. Point Pelee is beaches, forests and marsh. Each of these environments blends subtly into the next. At each transition, life is an interesting combination of elements of both worlds. The Park is an example of the forest popularly called Carolinian, which once covered nearly all of southern Ontario. Point Pelee lies near the northern limit of this forest, which is typical of central eastern North

America. Many of the tree species found at Point Pelee National Park have their southern range limits in the American states of South Carolina and Arkansas. Some species of plants and animals may be found as far south as Mexico and Central America.

Point Pelee is many things to many people. The region has had a long and interesting association with man. From early native encampments, to explorers, to soldiers, to squatters, to sailors, to fishermen, to farmers, to recreationalists, naturalists and all other visitors in the Park, Point Pelee has probably been more affected by man than any other National Park in Canada.

As early as the mid 1930s, 250,000 visitors entered into the Park each year. Usage peaked in the late '60s at 760,000 visitors. Today, approximately 350,000 people visit Point Pelee National Park annually: still an enormous guest list for such a confined nature preserve. Point Pelee pre-

> 66 The Point, even as it is now, is awfully important to people around here as well as to the tourists coming in to see the things that the Park still has to offer. It is something remarkable. The 'bird people' coming from all over the world are aware of this particular spot anyway and then they learn about the rest of Canada. 99
>
> **Marion Bridgman**
> Former Park Resident.

ON THE 42ND PARALLEL: From a southerly perspective, Point Pelee is where mainland Canada begins. Perched on the 42nd parallel – somewhat south of the mid-way point between the North Pole and the equator – Point Pelee shares its line of latitude with Rome, Chicago, Barcelona, the northern boundary of California, northern Turkey and northern Japan.

serves a unique sandspit formation, a southern Great Lakes marsh, and an example of the northern hardwood forest in Canada. Vines are a dimension of the forest which serve to emphasize its southern nature. Many of the plants found at Point Pelee are seldom found further north in North America. With more than 750 species of plants within its boundaries, Point Pelee is indeed a challenge for the botanist. The sheer numbers of plant and animal life serve as a testament

to the tremendous complexity of life at Point Pelee National Park.

For many visitors, the beaches that rim the sandspit and the quiet shady forest provide relief from city summer life. But perhaps as its signature, Point Pelee is one of the world's most famous locations for watching the migrations of both birds and insects. It is located on both the Atlantic and Mississippi flyways, and at the apex of the southern Ontario peninsula which funnels birds and insects through Point Pelee. As of 2002, more than 360 species of birds have been sighted at Point Pelee. Thousands of Monarch butterflies and dragonflies migrate from Point Pelee each fall as well. It was the turn of the 20th century when Point Pelee was first recognized as being a concentration point for migratory birds by noted ornithologists. In 1915 P. A. Taverner, then the Dominion Ornithologist, wrote: "Point Pelee forms one of the most important migration highways in America." Taverner recommended that Point Pelee be preserved as a national sanctuary. On May 29, 1918 his vision became reality when Point Pelee was proclaimed a National Park, the ninth park in the system and the first to be created on the merit of its ecological values.

Basking in the Bounty

The town of Leamington and Point Pelee National Park are often cited by visitors to the area in the same sentence. Situated just north of the Park, Canada's most southern town enjoys a region of Ontario where rare plant and animal species flour-ish, where the rich land grows the most diverse range of crops in Canada, where naturalists from around the world flock to witness the spectacular migration of birds and monarch butterflies, where seniors choose to spend their retirement years and

where breathtaking sunsets, secluded beaches, fine dining, after-supper sails and friendly faces are a way of life. The population of Leamington is a rich mix of nationalities – all of which add to the appeal of this busy community. A mosaic of ethnic clubs, restaurants, flags and monuments throughout the area offer visitors and locals alike the chance to immerse themselves in a variety of cultures from around the globe.

It has been said that if it doesn't grow in Leamington, it doesn't grow anywhere in Canada! Renowned as "The Tomato Capital" of Canada, the area produces a multitude of crops grown not only to supply the local processing industries, but the omnipresent roadside fruit and vegetable stands as well. With more than 800 acres "under glass" – 70 percent of Ontario's greenhouse industry – fresh produce is always in abundant supply. Tomatoes, cucumbers and flowers – a flourishing floral industry specializing in roses, bedding plants and seasonal blooms – are the main greenhouse crops but asparagus, beans, sweet corn, onions, lettuce, celery, carrots, zucchini, peppers, melons, squash and potatoes, decorate the local landscape as well. Fruits of all types also abound: peaches, grapes, apples and strawberries are all grown locally. The throughways of Leamington are also avenues of the Canada South Wine Route, a collection of lush country vineyards and wineries, some large and others quaint.

Apart from the agricultural diversity, the waters of Lake Erie are a fisherman's dream. Local fisheries have instituted retail outlets, selling their fresh catch of the day. Leamington's waterfront is alive with activity in the summertime, from pleasure boating and wind-surfing to swimming, sunning and strolling. The Municipal Marina and the lakeside promenade are exquisite additions to the shoreline development, serving as a launch to the Erie Islands by private craft or by ferry.

Leamington's "ErieQuest" diving development project has identified over 50 shipwrecks in the area, offering some fascinating insight into the rich nautical history of the Pelee Passage, and gathering wide enthusiasm and activity from across North America.

SEASONAL EFFECT. Point Pelee National Park lies within a climate zone classified as humid continental. Weather is strongly influenced by seasonal conflict between polar and tropical air masses. The climate of southwestern Ontario is one of the most versatile in Canada. Lake Erie greatly modifies the climate. In autumn, lake waters cool more slowly than the land and in spring, the land warms faster than the water, thereby extending the growing season and making the Leamington area the most frost-free of all Ontario.

The Lake Erie Archipelago

Point Pelee is one link in a series of stepping stones that stretch across Lake Erie. Together with the lake's western basin islands – Pelee, Hen, Middle, the Bass Islands and Kelley's Island – an incomplete land bridge is formed with the peninsula of Marblehead, Ohio, the adjacent mainland on the south shore of Lake Erie. It is believed that a more pronounced bridge once existed, making lake crossings feasible for Aboriginal canoeists. Sections of open water were smaller, and shelter from unpredictable storms was near at hand. A well travelled route between the Point Pelee peninsula and Marblehead made for many cultural similarities among the peoples of the two regions.

This travel route was not used exclusively by human migrants. Through the ages, the chain of islands between the peninsulas has made migration possible for small birds. The islands could become resting places or shelter in storms when necessary. Point Pelee has always been an important constituent of the Lake Erie Archipelago.

Native Peoples at Point Pelee

66 When the government took over the Point, my grandmother was forced to leave. She told me that they walked for miles and miles with their bundle of clothing and whatever they had. They were never given another piece of land, so they were nomads. The Caldwell Indians became widespread; they're over in the States, in northern and southern Ontario.

My great-grandfather was a chief of the Pottawatomi tribe; we were on the Island (Pelee) and at the Point. The whole thing was theirs; they fished and hunted the whole area. They were driven out of the Point in the 1880s, but some families came back after World War I and lived there until the '20s. They lived in rented houses but it wasn't their land anymore. And they were discriminated against from that day to this.

My ancestors were considered savages. They were not savages; they were just fighting for their lives. They were fighting to keep what they felt they owned. 99

Mildred Ford Date of Birth 1923. A member of the Caldwell Indian Band. Her grandmother, Mary Jane Dodge, was driven out of the Point in the late 1800s.

Roughly 1,000 years before the epic voyage of Christopher Columbus, Point Pelee had its earliest known inhabitants. About AD 500 – approximately 500 years before Norse adventurers discovered North America – Aboriginal peoples were hunting and gathering at Point Pelee, with particular interest in the marsh, as it was a storehouse of edible plants, fish and animal life.

There is evidence of three major periods of occupation before AD 1100, each sharing a common feature: the inhabitants stayed only for the late spring, summer and fall months. The lack of evidence of migratory bird species found in scattered bones around the sites suggests that the camps were built and abandoned after and before migration.

Pottery is an important clue to the origin and culture of the inhabitants. Pot shards found at Point Pelee suggest a fairly complex culture for the area with similar influences found in groups from Michigan and northern Ohio. The main connection, however, is with groups from upper New York State, particularly near Buffalo.

Point Pelee was a focal point for Aboriginal trails in the area. Some of the major highways in Essex County today had their origins as trails. There also seemed to be a route from Point Pelee to Sandusky, Ohio, where canoeists would traverse the lake through the shelter of the island groups.

The name for Lake Erie came from the early inhabitants of the southern shore. These were the *Lake Erie Indians*, a fiercely arrogant and proud people. Their name comes from the Iroquois word, Erige, meaning "cat" or "panther". Thus, they became known as the "people of the Cat". Early French maps titled Lake Erie as "Lac du Chat" or Lake of the Cat. In 1645, the Eries lost an athletic contest to the Iroquois people. A resulting war eventually ended with the complete decimation of the Cat people.

In May of 1788, Pelee Island and Point Pelee were leased from the Chippewa and Ottawa peoples. The lease was to extend for 999 years, for three bushels of corn annually for each area. The leasees were James Allen and Joseph Caldwell for Point Pelee, with Caldwell signing for Thomas McKee of Pelee Island. However, in a treaty in 1790, all of the Point Pelee land was given back to the Crown; half became part of the British Naval Reserve. The native peoples continued to live at Point Pelee and in 1882 renewed their claims to the region because of the promised land grants for service in the War of 1812. A British surgeon by the name of Smith visited Point Pelee in 1899, stating in his journal that about 100 Chippewa grew corn and oats there, and hunted and fished in Lake Erie.

In 1922, descendants of the indigenous families living at Point Pelee in the late 1700s claimed ancestral rights, and squatted on the land. They felt that by a treaty of 1749 – treaties in those years tended to lack the clarity of later agreements – they were in possession of the area. Reminded of a 1790 treaty that discounted their petition, an assembly of 300 Aboriginals from up-river Walpole Island planned an invasion. The Royal Canadian Mounted Police were dispatched to prevent trouble, and the invasion never came.

The work of archaeologists has been invaluable in helping reconstruct history. Trash heaps and bone piles of native encampments at the Point have proven to be treasure troves of information. Excavations have shown that wildlife at Point Pelee and the surrounding area was even more diverse than it is today. It is also understood that Point Pelee's early occupants were a proud and inventive people whose story is largely told by the soil.

Steamer "St. Louis" #1

Pigeon Cr.
Union Leamington
Ruthven 76·77·78
Dock 79·80
81·82
PIGEON 207
BAY

177
178

181

131·151A·152
153·154·155
156·157·158
159·160·161
162·163·164
165·166·167
168·169·170
171·172·173
174·175·176
202

206
A·B·C
198 Pelee Pt.
Grubb Reef
Dummy Lite
208·146·147
148·149·150

205

PELEE
134 135 136 137 138
133

142
143·144

128
Lighthouse Pt. 127 Middle Ground Shoal
126
122 123
124 125
210
129
130·131
PASSAGE

Southeast Shoal
140·141
139·209

182

Pelee Is.

Mill Pt.

W

Chickenolee Reef
115

ito Pt.
120
Fish Pt. 121
118·119

112 114
Middle Is.
113·114·117

Exploration

As early explorers found their way around Point Pelee, the sandspit was merely a reference point on the developing highway of the Great Lakes. It was also a warning for sailors of the dangerous shallows and currents offshore. For them, there was no great source of wealth to be found at the Point. Rich trapping grounds lay to the north. Minerals are not mined in sand. The sandy soil was a last choice for farming, since the rich clay and loam of the nearby mainland had much more appeal. Lake Erie was one of the last Great Lakes to be discovered, since early explorers and fur traders used more northerly routes.

The first white men to come to Point Pelee were two Sulpician priests: Fathers Dollier de Casson and De Brehant de Galinee. In 1669, Robert Cavalier de la Salle planned to go to the southwest, to explore the Ohio River. He thereby expected to get to the South Sea, and thence to China. Dollier and Galinee joined the expedition to record the journey's events.

Their campaign left on July 5, 1669 from Montreal with twenty-one men and seven canoes. They travelled up the St. Lawrence River and along Lake Ontario's south shore. Along the way, they met a man named Joliet, who had been commissioned to explore the Lake Superior region. Joliet had just come through a new route from Lake Huron to Lake Erie, and spoke about the route. Joliet also told Dollier about a tribe of natives, the Potawatomi in the north, who had not been visited by a missionary. Dollier wished to work among them. LaSalle's party split up into two groups. Taking seven men and three of the canoes, Dollier and Galinee set out for Lake Erie by way of the Grand River. They followed the northern shore of Lake Erie to present-day Port Dover, where they wintered. On March 23, 1670, they set out again, landing three days later at Point Pelee.

The name Point Pelee came from the early French who landed on the point and named the area Pointe Pelée, meaning "bare" or "bald", alluding to the fact that the area was devoid of vegetation. In 1721, Pierre Francois Xavier Charlevoix, a Jesuit, visited the French colonies in America. In his journal of his trip, he tells of his experience at Point Pelee: "On the fourth (of June) we spent a good part of the day on a point which runs north and south three leagues and which is called Pointe Pelée. It is however well enough wooded on the west side but the east side is a sandy tract of land with nothing but red cedars that are quite small and not in abundant quantity. There are a great number of bear in this part of the country and last winter more than four hundred were killed on Pointe Pelée alone."

Between 1689 and 1763, England and France engaged in a series of wars, both on the European continent and in North America. The conflict in North America developed as a question of possession of the colonies. The war on this continent ended with the capture of Montreal by the English on September 7, 1760. A formal peace was not signed until 1763. However, with the capture of Montreal, an English force was sent to occupy Detroit, the most important French post inland.

During the war, several Aboriginal tribes around the Great Lakes fought for their French allies. The native peoples retained a resentment against the English, and in 1763, Pontiac, an Ottawa chieftain, planned to take all of the interior forts out of

English hands for the French. He planned to lead the attack on Detroit himself. Pontiac had hoped that the French inhabitants would join him, but did not know that the treaty to end the war had already been signed in Paris. All French settlers had been made British subjects by the treaty, and could have been charged with treason if they joined Pontiac's force. There was no chance that France could come to Pontiac's aid.

Pontiac had planned to launch his raid on May 7, 1763, the day on which all British posts were to be attacked. His plan was discovered, however, and the British were ready when his braves crossed the river. The sloop *Michigan*, anchored at the mouth of the Detroit River, gave Pontiac the inclination that provisions or reinforcements were expected at the fort. A band of native peoples was sent along the north shore of Lake Erie to intercept any parties coming from Niagara.

Lieutenant Abraham Cuyler, with 96 members of Captain Hopkins's Independent Company, the Queen's Rangers, accompanied by 15 men of the Royal American Regiment, approached from Fort Niagara. The group was sent with provisions for Fort Detroit, stopping to camp at Point Pelee for a night en route. Pontiac's Wyandot braves attacked. In the sudden assault, Cuyler quickly formed his men into a semi-circle around the boats. Pontiac's men opened fire, and rushed the vessels. Some of Cuyler's men returned fire, but most panicked, throwing down their guns and fleeing to the boats. Five boats were pushed off, and headed into the lake. The natives captured three of them. Cuyler found himself abandoned by his men, but succeeded in reaching one of the two boats that stole away.

Fighting continued in and around Point Pelee until late the following fall (1764), ending when the Aboriginals' supplies ran low and with the realization that French aid would not come.

> The only ones who could trap were the ones who lived on the Point. No outsiders could come in. We trapped mostly muskrat, and sometimes mink or an occasional raccoon. Each person had 50 traps a piece, and if you'd catch them all full of rats everyday, then it was alright. We'd get out there about eight o'clock in the morning and start pulling rats up (from the traps). The pelts were sold to buyers from Detroit, New York, Toronto, and even Montreal.
>
> **Ersell Ashton**
> Former Park Resident. Date of Birth circa 1900.

The DeLaurier Trail (1.25 kilometres) meanders through reclaimed farmland. It features two historic buildings dating back to the 1840s, plus exhibits on the history of Point Pelee.

> 66 My grandfather bought that property for about twenty five cents an acre, I believe. My father farmed and fished. They used to take the fish across in sailboats to Sandusky and sell them to the Coast Fish Company. In later years, he sent the fish tug – he had two – to pick up all the fish along the shore. 99
>
> **Roy DeLaurier** Date of Birth 1893. Former Park Resident. Descendant of the original DeLaurier family.

Settlement and Development

The great potential for agriculture in southwestern Ontario was realized in the early 1800s, but tension and unrest in the years before 1812 between the Americans and British hindered settlement and development in the Western Lake Erie region. During the War of 1812, a man by the name of Parisien tells of problems at Point Pelee. The Americans were stopping supply ships making passage to Fort Amherstburg (present day Fort Malden in Amherstburg). When rounding Point Pelee, the ships were exposed to fire from American ships. He claimed that together, the

guns and the shoals at Point Pelee made passage difficult.

After the war ended in 1814, the land was "opened up." Construction of the Talbot Road provided a land-link along Lake Erie's north shore to young towns and cities. Packet boats provided transportation between shoreline communities. Villages and towns sprang up as the agricultural industry grew. The wealth in this area lay in the productivity of the land.

Among the first white settlers at Point Pelee were the DeLauriers in 1834. Their log house still stands in the Park today. The house appears to have been built mainly from trees in the immediate area of the building, a monument to the forest life in the early 1800s.

During its history, the family home served as a private residence and also as an inn for travellers, predominantly for those from Pelee Island who operated the Ironclad sleigh service from the Island to the Point. At one time, early in automotive history, a gas pump stood near the road. The DeLaurier family was involved in subsistence farming, with a love of exotic plants. The Charles DeLaurier family also operated a fishery on the west beach near the house about the turn of the century.

Subsistence farming, fishing and trapping were major occupations at Point Pelee throughout the preponderance of its human history. Land was cleared and drained for farming. A canal system, to serve for irrigation of the farms, was developed in the early 1900s. Now that farming at Point Pelee is over, the fields and orchards are gradually returning to their natural state. The process of succession refers to the way in which different types of plants appear in a very predictable and orderly sequence. Plants that require bare soil and full sunlight are found first. Their shade provides refuge for plants that cannot tolerate harsh, open conditions. Gradually, the soil develops, the shade is more complete, and new plant species emerge. A forest develops from the field.

It is quite likely that Point Pelee figures in its region's lumbering history. A sawmill, located just north of the present Park, presumably handled logs from Point Pelee. Red cedar logs, because they resist decay, were a popular commodity for fence posts, and were plentiful on the Point. The dry forests of Point Pelee produced many species of trees prized for their wood. Black walnut, chestnut and red oak, tulip, elm and white ash were among the Point's most sought-after timbers.

A Lake's Harvest

Many of the commercial fisheries at Point Pelee were established near the end of the 19th century. From the records that exist today, it appears that there was a total of eleven fisheries operating from the Park area over the course of this industry's history within the Point. The first was established around 1830, and the last ceased operations in 1969.

The commercial fishing industry in Lake Erie began in 1815 with the suppression of British and American tensions after the war. Lake Erie had tremendous potential for a freshwater fishing industry. The varying depths of the lake's basins, the reefs and shoals, the warm water, and the nutrient flow made for a thriving and diverse population of fish. Still today, a greater variety of fish exists in Lake Erie than in any other of the Great Lakes.

The development of the commercial fishing industry at Point Pelee was a natural extension of the area's budding business. The Point served as an exceptional base for fishermen, considering that the nearby shoals were favoured by fish. As well, the sandy broad shoreline at the Point made Lake

Erie accessible, while the steep clay bluffs along much of the rest of the lake made it nearly impossible to access. Small boats, not needing the protection of a harbour, were used from the beaches.

Aboriginal peoples were the first fishermen on Lake Erie to use nets; they fished in sheltered marshes and bays around the lake. Their nets were often trapping enclosures, made of plant fibre, and anchored with carved stone net sinkers, which are

The Krause fishery moved to nearby Sturgeon Creek in 1969, ending commercial fishing within the Park's boundaries.

> The grocery wagon used to come along once or twice a week, and drive the Point and back. You'd buy your spices and stuff like that from the grocery wagon. It'd sell the same stuff as a medicine man might.
>
> **Foster Jackson** Park Enthusiast. Date of Birth 1892.

still today occasionally found on the beaches.

One of the earliest methods of commercial fishing in the area used pound nets to entrap fish. Long heavy stakes were driven into the lake bottom to support the nets. The netting, leading out from shallow water near shore to deeper water, were hung on the stakes. Long arms of the meshed apparatus directed fish into an enclosure, where they remained alive and fresh until lifted into boats.

In the 1850s, improved engines (steam-powered) and watercraft moved the fishing industry from the shore and extended it throughout the entire lake. By 1872 the federal government had surveyed the waters surrounding the Pelee peninsula into water lots and leased them to commercial

fisheries. In 1891 some 22 fishery licenses were issued in and around Point Pelee.

In the late 1860s, a sturgeon fishery was established by European immigrants. The "nouveau" fishery smoked the grand fish, extracted its oil, manufactured caviar from its eggs and made isinglass (jelly) from its air bladder. (Prior to this enterprise, the Sturgeon was considered a nuisance fish, often being used for fertilizer and for burning in the boilers of steamships.) Soon after, buildings and net drying compounds were constructed at the Point for the processing of Sturgeon. By 1900, Sturgeon was nearly eliminated from the lake.

Other species began to be fished intensely – Lake Trout, Lake Whitefish and Lake Herring – and shortly after 1900 these species, too, slowly declined in numbers. Intensive and selective fishing as well as habitat destruction – damming, shore erosion, nutrient loading and the invasion of new species – were all contributors to their demise. Lake Trout were eliminated by the late 19th century and by 1929 the Lake Herring (Cisco) and Northern Pike virtually disappeared.

By the 1940s sport fishing became an important activity, and in the early 1950s a period of great instability in the Lake Erie fish population occurred due to non-selective and intensified fishing. By the 1960s the species composition of Lake Erie had changed considerably.

Coming of Age

Theory holds that after the last ice age, Point Pelee and extreme southwestern Ontario comprised a migration route for plants and animals. In a warming trend, the ice melted away. Plant and animal life moved north to colonize the land freed from the ice. For some thousands of years, water levels in the newly formed Great Lakes were unsettled.

At one stage, the West Basin of Lake Erie was smaller and shallower than at present. Land bridges across the islands and peninsulas south of Point Pelee, and at the west end of the lake, were nearly complete. Plant and animal invasions via the land bridges, and aided by post-glacial warming trends, took place.

Plant Life

Point Pelee held a particular fascination for groups of biologists and naturalists in the years adjoining the turn of the 20th century. Each investigator, through his or her own field of study, became impressed with the rich variety of life. Members of the Great Lakes Ornithological Club, studying bird

life and migration at Point Pelee in the early 1900s, made several references to the southern types of plants in their notes. They were so intrigued by their discoveries that they encouraged C.K. Dodge to publish a list of plants found at Point Pelee. Dodge's work was completed in 1914 with a listing

of 583 species for Point Pelee, 408 species for Pelee Island and on both, 623 species. Forty species found on the Island were not at Point Pelee.

Plant life at Pelee poses many interesting questions for the botanist. There are many southern plant species, and yet there are northerly and westerly species as well. Several species common to Pelee are rare elsewhere in Ontario, while species of the surrounding area are not always present at Point Pelee. Keys to understanding these situations lie in understanding the geographical associations of this area.

A name popularized to describe the forest type of central eastern North America is "Carolinian". Point Pelee lies just south of the northern limit of this forest type. The southern limit of this zone incorporates regions of North and South Carolina, and Kentucky.

Designated a wetland of international significance (RAMSAR Convention, 1987), Point Pelee's marsh is one of the few left on the Great Lakes.

The tree composition of Point Pelee National Park is markedly different from that in the surrounding province and numerous species occur at the Point which are not found much further north. The Tulip tree, Black Oak, Blue Ash, Pawpaw, Red Mulberry, White Sassafras, Black Walnut, Sycamore and Chestnut Oak are examples of trees that occur in Canada only in the Carolinian forest of southern Ontario. Representative shrubs which are restricted to the Point Pelee region are Spicebush, Redbud, Burning Bush and Drummond's Dogwood. Herbs which are restricted to the region are Burgrass, Sand Grass, Swamp Rose Mallow, Prickly Pear Cactus, Wild Potato Vine and Flowering Spurge. Together, these southern species, the lush growth and the abundant hanging vines give the Park's vegetation an appropriate "southern look". To date, approximately seven hundred species of plants have been identified at Point Pelee. This is a substantial number, considering that the Park is less than 16 square kilometres in area.

66 **The first Mountie came down here walking. Every Sunday he'd dress up – a fellow by the name of Al Kupke - with the big leather boots and spurs. It's hot in the summer here you know. He had his crown hat on, big tunic, and people would pull right up beside him on the road and just look with awe. 'There's a Mountie,' they'd say. He was the real McCoy.** 99

Cecil Balkwill Born at the Park on May 18, 1923.

Animal Life

Man, throughout his existence, has been greatly dependent upon animal life. Some animals have served man directly... as food, as pets and as sources of power and transportation. Some have troubled man, threatening his flocks and crops, or as predators to man himself. There are a great many animals with which man has no direct dealing, but yet on which man must rely for the health and well being of his world. Throughout history, man has brought many changes to animal populations of the world. In the southern Ontario region, over the past one thousand years, animal populations have been altered to a significant degree. Relationships between man and the

land at Point Pelee may serve to illustrate man-made change.

Archaeologists, exploring the Park in recent decades, have made great contributions to the knowledge of animal life at Point Pelee in the past. Their findings have shown that some animal life at Point Pelee in centuries past is not present today. Elk, black bear, wild turkey, chipmunk, passenger pigeon and beaver are no longer found in the Park area. In part, changes in populations of large animals at Point Pelee were brought about by changes in man's treatment of the land. The land's first human inhabitants were Aboriginal peoples. Archaeological findings show that they were hunters, camping on the sandspit during the summer months. Before AD 1000, very little agriculture was practiced; the land was hunted. Extensive woods and marshes supported large and diverse animal populations; fish were plentiful in the lake and marsh.

European settlers brought great and rapid change to animal populations by changing their habitat. Agriculture was, and still is today, a prosperous venture in this area of Ontario, with level land and rich soil facilitating the development of farmland. Refuge for many animals was lost, as cover and food plant populations were reduced. As well, in early days of settlement, domestic animals were scarce; wild game often satisfied the demand for meat. Settlers' firearms proved to be far more efficient at taking game than were the traps and bows of the native peoples. The American elk, black bear, white-tailed deer, beaver and wild turkey disappeared from Point Pelee.

Extensive areas of marsh north of the Park were drained for farming and subsequently the wildlife dependent on marshes was reduced. Lake Erie, with the pressure of the fishing industry, and changes in water chemistry, underwent radical changes in its population structure as well.

Feathered Guests

Numerous factors contribute to Point Pelee's use by migrating birds. Night migrants, which may have flown for hours in the cover of darkness, usually look for a suitable place to land at daybreak. If at this time they are over the lake they will see Point Pelee as one of the first places offering a landing point with their desired habitats. The diverse range of habitats, from lake to beach

> 66 It was often humourous – but sometimes hazardous – the reactions of birdwatchers who appeared in great numbers in the spring of the year. They would often abandon their vehicles without warning should a species of interest be suddenly spotted. The unwary and unlucky driver behind such a group may not have the same interest and would find himself a statistic on a police officer's accident report. Fortunately, only feelings and fenders were hurt. 99
>
> **S/Sgt. R.R. Thomson** Royal Canadian Mounted Police 1970.

31

to forest to savannah to marsh, encourages many types of birds to stop a while and "fuel up" for another long migratory flight.

Day migrants follow landform and may be funnelled to pass through Point Pelee. This is the situation in the fall with Sharp-shinned Hawks and Blue Jays, which some days pass over the Park in great numbers.

From the tip of the Point, birds can be seen "jumping off" and flying out over the lake. American Bitterns can be found in the grass near the tip as they wait for darkness to continue their flights northward. The pervading atmosphere is one of urgency yet calm resolution when the migration swings into high gear. Flocks gather and congregate. Two hundred and fifty thousand Red-winged Blackbirds have been estimated in the marsh at one time and offshore, hordes of Red-breasted Mergansers often stretch across the horizon as far as the eye can see. Overhead, flocks of Blue Jays stretch for kilometres like a column of living smoke. Occasionally, in spring, reverse migration is witnessed when birds originally heading north reverse their direction and return south presumably because of an insufficient source of food at the Point.

Winter birds at the Park can number between 60 and 110 species, a normal number for the southern Ontario region, but Point Pelee is of particular winter bird interest insofar as it lies near the northern edge of the winter ranges of such birds as Rufous-sided Towhee, Eastern Bluebird, Brown Thrasher and Vesper Sparrow.

Breeding birds number almost 100 species and of those, the resident Carolinian birds are most noteworthy: the Yellow-breasted Chat, Orchard Oriole, Blue-grey Gnatcatcher and Chuck-will's Widow. Resident marsh birds are of interest as well. Black Terns, Least Bitterns, Marsh Wrens and Common Gallinules nest in the marsh.

The Migrations

Point Pelee National Park is renowned as the best location in inland North America to observe the northward migration of songbirds. The guest registry in the Park's Visitor Centre shows that birders come from far and wide to experience this special event. Almost half are from outside Canada – the majority of these from the United States. Mid-May at Point Pelee has become a birding festival welcoming tens of thousands of enthusiasts celebrating the return of the spring birds.

Arguably, the most impressive aspect of Point Pelee's spring migration is the diversity and colos-

sal numbers of northbound warblers that descend on the Park, affording the area the reputation of the "Warbler Capital of North America." Point Pelee is perfectly situated. It is far enough north so as to receive the warbler collectives flying only through Texas as well as those flying only through Florida. Yet, it is also far enough south to attract the "southerners" such as Hooded, Kentucky and Worm-eating Warblers.

The stream of birds in the spring is not a steady flow from the south. The birds usually arrive in intermittent waves, a pattern unique to eastern North America. A "wave" occurs as a result of a warm weather front advancing from the south or southeast meeting a cold weather front from the north or northwest. Two situations will cause the birds to descend. One is when the two fronts meet at ground level. The other is when a warm front in which migrating birds are flying overrides a cold front. The rising warm air becomes cooler with the increasing altitude until it is finally too cold for the birds and they descend.

When nocturnal (night-time) migrants find themselves over Lake Erie near sunrise they must continue onwards or drown. After flying perhaps hundreds of kilometres in one night it is this extra 30 to 40 kilometres (18 to 25 miles) across the lake that really demands their last strength. This explains why completely exhausted birds are sometimes found at the Point's tip.

With the onset of increasingly shorter days that announces the coming of autumn, it is once again a time of abundant bird life at Point Pelee National Park. With the overall population of birds in North America greatly swelled by the raising of young, the vast numbers that can be seen at Point Pelee during the impressive fall migration usually far outweigh the tallies from even the best of spring migrations.

The fall migration is distinct from the spring

journey in other ways as well. Unlike spring, when most species are brilliantly coloured and singing vigorously, the autumn migrants are generally dull plumaged and, except for call notes, usually silent. Nonetheless, the fall flight of most species is a less hurried affair than the frenzied northbound movement of the birds some months earlier.

The fall voyage is evident in some species of birds as early as the end of June and can still be witnessed as late as mid-December. Remarkably, the Yellow-rumped Warblers and the Greater Yellowlegs have fall migration periods covering four and five months respectively. Extended migration intervals allow even the most casual observer to study species otherwise "missed" during the spring cycle. For example, the Golden Eagle, Peregrine Falcon, Red-necked Phalarope, Northern Saw-whet Owl, Jaegers, Long-billed Dowitcher, and Stilt and Buff-breasted Sandpiper make for very rare sightings in the spring, but can be found with regularity during the fall season. The total number of bird species recorded at Point Pelee is 372, the majority of which have been first identified during the fall migration period.

Not unlike the spring, the arrival of the migrants in the fall often occurs in intermittent waves, with nocturnal birds showing the greatest movement toward the Park an hour or so before dawn as they search for suitable habitat for feeding and resting. The diurnal (day-time) migrants arrive in a different manner. It seems that they come south until they reach Lake Erie, then turn westward or eastward and follow the curvature of the shoreline to arrive at Point Pelee. By using Point Pelee as a stop-over station, the flight across the lake is certainly shortened, and the necessity of flying over open water is deferred for a time. But not all diurnal migrants fly south off the tip of the Park. Bobolinks, Broad-winged and Red-tailed Hawks, vultures, falcons and eagles are hesitant to cross

open water, and generally go further inland to go around, rather than cross, the lake. Blue Jays, in particular, rarely cross the lake due to vulnerability over water. The tens of thousands of Jays that fill the tip's October skies nearly all head along the shoreline seeking a safer route. This "dead-end" phenomenon is a mystery to many unassuming observers.

Mammals

Most of the mammals found in the Park are year-long residents. Like all other animals, mammals are an integral part of their environment, and are adapted to exploit the particular environment in which they live. For mammals, Point Pelee is isolated almost as if it were an island. To the north of the Park lie dyked and open farmland, and an extensively developed cottage area. The lake, on the remaining two sides of the triangular sandspit, is a barrier for all but the bats. There is very little movement by animals in and out of the Park. It is a rare occasion to see deer, coyotes, fox, rabbits, skunks or weasels entering or leaving the Park.

Man's use of the land in Point Pelee National Park imposes restrictions on the mammal population as well. Roadways, parking lots and building sites tend to limit movement of some animals. There are physical environmental limits to distribution. The marsh may prove to be a barrier to movement by some terrestrial mammals. On a smaller scale, open fields prove to be a barrier to woodland mice, while the opposite is generally true of the meadow vole. Because of great variations within beach, forest and marsh environments, there is a diverse mammal population, and interesting patterns of distribution in the Park.

Amphibians and Reptiles

Since 1895, there have been 30 species of reptiles and amphibians recorded in Point Pelee National Park. The lower Great Lakes-St. Lawrence Valley region has a more diverse population of these animals than any other part of Canada. A mild climate, with warm summers, and a rich variety of habitat account for the numerous species. Some species once found at Point Pelee have vanished over the years. Changes in the Park, such as the aging of the marsh and forest, and a natural regeneration of old fields may be reason enough to cause change. Unfortunately, when the populations fall to very low numbers, or disappear, the isolated nature of the Park – bound by farmland and the lake – inhibits replenishment from any surrounding surviving populations.

Fish of Lake Erie

Lake Erie, the shallowest and perhaps the most productive of the Great Lakes, has had 138 species of fish recorded from its waters. Visitors to Point Pelee may experience a few of the lake's fishes in close encounters only by those that wash ashore. Of the myriad of fish recorded, interest is usually focused on those few that are of commercial or sport fishing value. However, the sundry of "anonymous" and usually quite small species are very important to the ecological workings of the lake as food for other fish and animal life, and as consumers of the minute life of the lake. Without them, the character of the lake would change.

Change is a key word in describing the populations of the prominent fish of the lake. The Lake Trout, Ciscos, Lake Whitefish, Sauger and Blue Walleye have virtually disappeared from Lake Erie while increases have occurred in Yellow Perch, White Bass, Rainbow Smelt and Fresh-water Drum. Commercial fishing, competition and predation from introduced species – Salmon and Lampreys – as well as toxic materials from industry, shoreline erosion and eutrophication have been responsible for these changes.

Fish of the Marsh

The diversity of fish in the Park's marsh is reduced from that in the lake, since the available fish habitat is confined to several shallow reedy ponds and channels. Water depths vary between one and three metres and, in summer, the ponds become a tangle of underwater vegetation. Most fish are types that have adapted to slow moving, warm waters and wide temperature fluctuations.

Twenty-six species of fish have been recorded in the Pelee Marsh. Several of these, most notably the Carp, are not native to Point Pelee and may have contributed to changes in native species' populations by increasing the turbidity of the ponds. The most abundant large species are Carp, Bowfin, Northern Pike, Largemouth Bass, Yellow Perch, Bluegill and Pumpkinseed.

Occasionally, late winter die-offs of fish occur (mainly Carp) because oxygen in the water under the ice is not replaced as it is used up. It is believed that the fish suffocate.

> 66 Fishing boats were slow, but they were an excellent disguise for hauling booze over to the Island and then taking it from there by some other means. 99
>
> **Hugh McCormick** Date of Birth 1917.

Insects

Insects far exceed all other terrestrial animals in number. Their short lifespan and great numbers per generation have allowed insects to adapt, during trial and error evolution, to practically all features of the world's environments. Several hundred thousand species have been described thus far – more than three times the number of species in the remainder of the animal kingdom. Populations often reach millions per acre.

One of the most widely acclaimed features of Point Pelee National Park is the migration of the Monarch Butterfly (Danaus plexippus). Each year these insects are funnelled by the Great Lakes barrier southward along the Ontario peninsula. Point Pelee, as the tip of that funnel, is a gathering place.

Many other insects migrate from Point Pelee, at about the same time as the Monarch. Swallowtails, Brush-footed Butterflies and the Solitary Paper Wasp display migration. Dispersal movements, or movement from one habitat to another, as with dragonflies, can also be seen.

47

Monarch Migration

For a few special days each autumn, Point Pelee is a temporary home to countless thousands of migrating Monarch butterflies. Although commonly observed roosting in trees in times of cold weather – warm weather can preempt a stop-over altogether – the Monarchs are never in the habit of lingering. Once favourable conditions present themselves – warmer temperatures and supportive winds – they forge on across Lake Erie toward their destination in the mountains of central Mexico some 3,000 kilometres (1,800 miles) away. The Pelee peninsula offers the shortest route across the lake. Point Pelee's shape funnels the Monarchs to its tip.

Why such a marathon journey for this insect? The answer lies in the Monarch's food plant. Milkweed is the only plant that Monarch caterpillars eat. It is believed that both milkweed and Monarchs evolved in the mountains of Mexico. As the milkweed adapted and its range extended, the Monarch followed. But milkweed is listed as a noxious weed in Ontario and many states, posing a serious threat to the butterfly. As milkweed plants are removed, so is the Monarch's only food source. If milkweed disappears, so will the Monarch.

At present, the Monarch migration cycle remains a mystery. Through the summer there are two or three generations of the butterfly raised in Ontario. From egg to adult takes only about a month. The generation that emerges in late summer is somehow triggered to become a migratory generation. This generation over-winters in Mexico and mates there in the early spring. On their way north, eggs are laid on fresh milkweed and the adult dies shortly thereafter. It may take several generations of Monarch offspring before northward-bound butterflies reach Canada in May. No Monarch makes the entire journey. The mystery lies in how they know where to go?

66 It was a beautiful Park, beautiful. But you couldn't park in here, there were too many people in here. They came from every state in the Union and every province in Canada. And this was the most beautiful tourist Park in Canada. 99

Jack Cleveland Former Park Resident. Date of Birth 1902. Worked in Windsor.

the Ostracods, the Copepods, the Water Fleas and the Sideswimmers – as they form the basis of the food chain of the marsh. A pail of water dipped, in summer, from the marsh boardwalk often will contain thousands of clear-bodied water fleas. Crayfish are the largest crustaceans at Point Pelee and are a favourite food for the Park raccoons. Perhaps the prettiest of the Park's crustaceans are the Fairy Shrimp, which hatch in the early spring and can be seen in the troughs in Tilden's Woods.

Snails are the most abundant mollusks at Point Pelee. Orb snails inhabit the moist forests. Another mollusk, the freshwater clam, is found both in the marsh and in the lake. Spiders are ubiquitous at Point Pelee. By late summer and fall, it is difficult to find any plant or tree that does not have a spider's web attached. Other invertebrates found at the Point include Millipedes, Centipedes, Nematodes, Flatworms, Hydras, Protozoans, Earthworms and many more.

Fossils

A beachcomber on Point Pelee's shores invariably notices the abundance of fossils in the washed up gravels. These are mineral casts of animal life from an ancient warm sea which deposited a layer of sediments under Point Pelee. These sediments, dated to the Devonian Period, outcrop in Lake Erie and on Pelee Island. Natural forces such as grinding by glacial ice have liberated fossils from these sediments to join the gravel deposits around the lake. Corals, sea lilies, brachiopods and occasionally clams are found at Point Pelee.

Other Invertebrates

Because of their diminutive composition, the difficulty in identifying them and their infinite numbers, invertebrates other than insects tend to be overlooked. However, they too are important life links in Point Pelee's natural environments. Of particular importance are the minute crustaceans –

The Pelee Passage

In 1856, the steamer *Northern Indian* burned off the shore of Point Pelee with a loss of more than 30 lives. The schooner, *New Brunswick*, was wrecked in a storm in shallows just west of Point Pelee in 1858 dropping a cargo of oak and walnut valued at $173,000 to the lake floor. On June 4th, 1891, the schooner *Fayette Brown* sank in the Pelee Passage, later removed by the government as it was a menace to navigation.

Altogether, over 100 ships sank, burned or ran aground on the shoals about Point Pelee, many carrying passengers and valuable cargo to the bottom. The accounts of ships that have been lost, and the hulks of wrecks on the bottom, have been a warning to captains of the treacherous shoals.

The shoals to the southeast of Point Pelee are, in fact, an underwater extension of the Point itself. Waves in Lake Erie have constantly eroded the shorelines. Over thousands of years, the lake currents and wave-generated shoreline currents have moved the eroded sand and clay along the shorelines and along the lake bottom.

Point Pelee and its shoals to the south exist today because of rocky outcrops in the lake. This durable limestone ridge extends southward across the lake, exposing itself at Pelee Island, Kelley's Island, Marblehead and Sandusky. Between Point Pelee and the island groups, the rock ridge does not reach the water's surface, but creates shallow water by slowing currents and forcing sediment loads to be dropped. Point Pelee, a sandspit, grew in size as the sediment on the lake bottom built up. The shoals developed as an extension of the sandspit. What's more, the sandy shallow bottoms of the shoals continually shift. Waves and currents in the lake alter the shape of the shoals and the depth of the water.

Today, navigation through this dangerous section of the lake has become quite safe. An automated lighthouse at Southeast Shoal and a radio beacon guide ships approaching the shoal through deeper water. Lights and buoys mark the Pelee Passage ensuring that ships make the turns. Lake and ocean-going ships of today have powerful engines to keep them on course.

In the early days of lake travel, matters were quite different. The Southeast Shoal lighthouse was not built until 1925. For some years, a light-ship was anchored on the shoal, but before the mid-1800s, there were no guides to navigation. Lumbering activities at Point Pelee led to an increased concern about shipwrecks. It was felt that the trees helped to reduce shipwrecks because the forest could be seen by sailors approaching shore. Due to increased ship traffic around the tip, a lighthouse was constructed by 1862 on a sub-merged reef four miles off the Point's tip.

The presence of the shoals and the Pelee Passage forced captains to run their ships through an obstacle course. But it was storms that proved most problematic. In the confines of the shoals and passages, there was no room to run before a storm. The first ships on the lake were sail-pow-ered; making the passage meant relying on fair winds. Early steam-powered ships lacked the pow-er of engines today. A top speed of eight to ten knots on a good day was reduced to only a frac-tion of the speed in a storm. High winds forced many ships aground. Older steamers were forced to fire their boilers to pressures beyond safe limits. In some, boilers exploded; in others, bearings overheated and caught fire, or sparks from the funnels set the upper deck in flames.

A large loss of life came with the burning of the steamer *Clarion* in 1909. The *Clarion* worked in conjunction with the Pennsylvania Railroad. On the eighth of December, a severe storm caught the *Clarion* in the Pelee area. Heavily laden with a car-go of flour, feed, coal and glucose, the ship made poor way against the storm. By evening the cap-tain was forced to fire the boilers to dangerous limits. A fire broke out below deck, setting the ship ablaze. At the time, the *Clarion* was within a mile of the lightship *Keuwaunee*, which was anchored at the Southeast Shoal. Four hours after the blaze started, the freighter *L.C. Hanna* came to the scene. After three attempts, the *Hanna's* cap-

tain pulled near enough for six men on the stern to jump to the freighter. The captain and twelve men had tried to reach the *Keuwaunee*, but never made it.

The sandsucker *Sand Merchant* was lost in a storm while trying to make a run from Point Pelee to the home port of Cleveland. Four-metre (13-foot) waves in high winds beat the stern of the ship, causing the sand cargo to slosh in the hold. The ship listed and swamped. Some lifeboats were capsized, and some of the men were pulled under the ship as it rolled. Other men drowned as they tired during the night. Rescue ships the next day found only seven men still clinging to the remain-ing lifeboats.

At present, there are nearly a dozen ships on the bottom near Point Pelee. Of these, two lie within one hundred metres of the shore. A small wooden hulled steamer lies in six metres (twenty feet) of water off the east beach. A freighter lies about 300 metres off the west beach. Others lie near the shoals.

Life Saving Station

In the late 1800s and early 1900s, most of the Point served as a Naval Reserve. In 1902, because of the noted treachery of Point Pelee, a life saving station was constructed at the tip of the Point to rescue sailors in distress. The station's first captain was Lewis Wilkinson, formerly a commercial fish-erman and a man with a keen sense of the lake's idiosyncrasies. In his inaugural year as a life-sav-ing volunteer, the *Grace C. Gribbie* was wrecked on a sandbar off Point Pelee in an April gale. Wil-kinson swam to the ship in icy water to rescue three men clinging to a hatch cover. It was this act of heroism for which Wilkinson was made captain of the life-saving team. During the winter months,

> ❝ I think our wage was about $250 or $275 a month and we got free rent. Outside of that we had to buy everything else. Fishermen only made $45 a month. But my gracious alive, at that time you could go downtown and buy all the groceries you could carry for $5. ❞
>
> **Ersell Ashton** Date of Birth circa 1900.
> Worked at the Life Saving Station around 1937.

Closely related to the pebble ridges are the drift-lines, where flotsam and debris carried in the water have been cast up on the beach. Plant matter, such as algae and cattails, and animal matter such as fish, feathers and dead insects form a compost to help enrich the sand. This organic matter is a nutrient for beach plants; it helps hold moisture for the plants and binds the sand.

Life on the open beach is uncertain. During storms, waves crash over the beach face, battering plant and insect communities. In summer, the sand can reach 46 degrees Celsius in the hot sun. Wind-whipped winter spray might cover the beach in an icy armour. Swimmers and sunbathers, if not careful, can trample pebble ridges and driftlines. Nonetheless, the beach is far from devoid of life. Even on the most storm-ravaged, people-trodden sections of beach, ants, tiger beetles and spiders will be found. Shorebirds, gulls, terns and crows will not pass up the food tossed by waves upon the shore. Many of the Park's rare plants can be found in this habitat.

Point Pelee's beaches have played a vitally important role in Canadian history. For many sailors, the long sandspits were warning of treacherous shoals further offshore. Point Pelee attained a reputation as one of the most dangerous passage points in the history of Great Lakes shipping. In the earliest days of man's account at Point Pelee, native peoples came for the summer to fish. Lake Erie, easily reached from the gentle shores, made for ideal fishing conditions, as fishermen in the 19th and 20th centuries were to discover. Point Pelee's beaches were desired campsites for early explorers, traders and military men.

with the station closed and Wilkinson off duty, he was recurrently called to rescue the mail carriers stranded on the ice between Leamington and Pelee Island. The station closed April 1940.

Park Habitats

The Beaches

Point Pelee National Park shoulders approximately 20 kilometres of beach. Perhaps more than any other environment of the Park, the beaches represent the one feature of Point Pelee that is constantly changing! The shape, width and incline of the beaches may be altered completely in just hours, given a change in the mood of Lake Erie.

The beach habitat might be described as a series of bands, running roughly parallel to the water's edge. Waves, lapping on the beach, build ridges of pebbles. The pebbles help collect drifting sand, providing refuge for insects and spiders.

The Grassland and Savannah

Small islands of grassland are scattered throughout the Park. Many were once agricultural lands used for orchards and crops. Others have developed behind the growing beaches. As succession occurs, these areas will gradually assume the character of the surrounding forest. Where conditions are the driest, change to forest will take the longest. Sun-loving plants will move in first, surviving until they prepare a richer shaded ground. Forest plants will then take over. During the intermediate stages, a savannah of grasses, sumac and cedars develops. Many of the old farm fields are now at this stage and, as such, are the prime Prickly Pear Cactus habitat in the Park. Low bushes and young trees provide excellent food and protection for deer, rabbits, voles, moles and thicket-loving birds, and of course, their predators as well.

The Swamp Forest

Point Pelee's swamp forest lies south of its marsh and in years of higher water levels in the lake, low areas between beach ridges, called slacks or troughs, are often flooded. In very low water years they may be dry. Accordingly, the swamp forest is extremely variable in its character.

Fallen trees are part of the character of the wet forest. In years when water levels are low, dry forest species of trees can invade. Water may suffocate the roots, killing these trees, if the water again becomes deeper. In time, the trees will fall – perhaps blown down by winds, or made top heavy by climbing vines. Root systems in the swamp forest are shallow to avoid wet sand below. In the 1950s the entire character of the swamp began to change. Dutch Elm disease ravished the elms in the swamp forest. Once dead, these trees became extremely susceptible to strong southwesterly winds, and many were toppled. Their intertwining root systems often resulted in a chain reaction. Flooding, due to high lake levels since the early 1970s, has drowned other trees.

Silver Maple and Sycamore are the main swamp forest "survivors". Jewelweed and nettles grow

profusely in the wet soil. Duckweed carpets the water in years when the slacks are flooded. To the human eye, this forest appears virtually impenetrable in summer months. Lush growth, abundant mosquitoes, and tangles of fallen vine-laden trees seem to block all passage. The Woodland Nature Trail however, provides visitors with access to this habitat. Although a hindrance to exploring man, the swamp forest environment is a haven to wildlife. Deer, coyotes, weasels and raccoons frequent the area. Wood ducks, night herons, wrens and thrushes are common. Fish, especially Bowfin and Carp, find their way into the flooded swamp forest; Spring Peepers and Grey Tree Frogs are heard, but seldom seen. Clues to this forest's animal life are prints in soft earth, or sounds from trees overhead. The wet forest is a true contrast to any other part of the Park – one greatly diverse in life.

The Dry Forest

The dry forest is not totally unlike the swamp forest. Although not as pronounced as in the wet woodlands, the beach ridges are still prevalent. The land is gently rolling, creating a variety of conditions in soil water, soil structure and lighting. Most of the dry forest is hardwood; Hackberry is by far the most common tree. Other hardwoods include White Ash, Basswood, Black Walnut, Shagbark Hickory, Sassafrass, Red Oak, Chestnut Oak, Chinquapin Oak and Sugar Maple to name a few. But while there are many species of trees, Point Pelee's forest is young and developing, and it remains to be seen in the years ahead which species will continue to survive in the changing forest.

A small part of the dry forest is predominantly pine, especially in the area of Black Willow Beach. The pine was considered an asset during Point Pelee's history as a Naval Reserve, in years before and just after the turn of the century; however, none was cut down for Naval purposes. Today, the pine forest is a favourite stopover for birds migrating to and from more northerly pine forests. Look to their treetops and the pines tell a story of the winds; dried by the prevailing winds on their west sides, the pines have been "flagged" toward the east.

The Marsh

The Point Pelee marsh occupies the northeastern two-thirds of the Park and covers an area of 10 square kilometres. The marsh is surrounded on three sides by permeable sand ridges and water slowly percolates back and forth from lake to marsh.

Four major plant associations have developed in the marsh. The cattail mat covers two-thirds of the marsh giving it its distinctive character somewhat reminiscent of the everglades. The success of the cattail mat is due, to some extent, to its ability to float up and down according to fluctuating water levels. Red-winged Blackbirds, Marsh Wrens, Yellowthroats, raccoons, mink, muskrats and a variety of plants and insects take advantage of this unusual environment.

Marsh ponds contain the second most abundant plant association in the marsh – a variable "soup" of waterlilies and underwater plants. Fish, turtles, ducks, aquatic insects and billions of microscopic creatures are part of the organization of life in this zone.

Buttonbush Carr, which rims the west side of the marsh, and "pockets" of Loosestrife-duckweed in the southern end of the marsh, do not cover much area but increase the opportunity for diversity for animal forms in the marsh.

Ecological Integrity

Like all National Parks, Point Pelee strives to protect its areas of natural significance for future generations. Point Pelee safeguards the Carolinian zone, which in Canada is restricted to the most southern part of Ontario, and is characterized by the presence of flora and fauna whose ranges extend far to the south. Many species that are representative of the Carolinian zone are rare, threatened or endangered in Canada. The Park's prime consideration in the planning, operation and management of Point Pelee is the maintenance of the ecological integrity of its Carolinian forest and southern Great Lakes marsh ecosystems.

Ecological integrity may best be described as an environmental puzzle with plants, animals, food webs, natural disturbances, nutrient cycles and people among its pieces. When all the pieces fit together undamaged, there is ecological integrity.

When a piece is removed – the extinction of a species perhaps – the picture changes. The more pieces that are damaged, or go missing, the more obscured the image becomes. Of course, the environment is dynamic and when one component is altered, others change and adapt. But the ecosystem has changed, sometimes in ways that are not detectable, other times in ways that cause considerable alteration to the puzzle picture.

" When I was young there really weren't a lot of tourists in the Park ... the only thing we had were those scientists who came from Toronto to catch butterflies. "

Annie Jackson Born at the Park in 1910. Moved to Leamington at age 12.

A Park for All Seasons

By J. Robertson Graham

To describe Point Pelee National Park with only one word, that word may be "diversity." One sees it in the different types of habitats, in the unusual mix of southern and northern species of plants and animals, and in the way people have used the Park. But that's not all. At Point Pelee, there is also a tremendous variety of ways that the Park can be enjoyed throughout all four seasons. From birding to bicycling to skiing, the changing seasons create perfect conditions for a wide range of activities.

The bird migration has made Point Pelee world-famous, setting it apart from all other national parks in Canada. Spring migration at Point Pelee begins as early as the end of January with the arrival of the Horned Larks. Then come the water-fowl: the ducks, geese and swans. By the end of March, many species of birds are making their appearance, including Common Flickers, Tree Swallows, Hermit Thrushes, Winter Wrens and Bonaparte's Gulls, to mention a few.

April sees the arrival of not only more birds, but a broadening of the variety of species as well: the early shorebirds, the herons, more swallows, a variety of woodpeckers, a smattering of rails, sparrows, some hawk species, more thrushes and the first warblers. Despite all of this exciting spring action, Point Pelee is best known for its songbird migration. In a typical year, the arrival of these birds moves into full swing in late April or early May, with its peak sometime towards the third week of May. The vociferous warblers are the highlight of the colourful songbird migration, considered by some as the "butterflies of the bird world." During the peak of the migration, seeing more

Threats to ecological integrity vary from park to park depending on the regional environment and history of the area in which they exist. Because of its location, Point Pelee National Park does not entirely represent the biogeographic zone to which it belongs and much of the original system has been considerably altered or destroyed in the last 200 years.

To counter these changes, the Park's management team has for many years been very active in the attempt to restore some of Point Pelee's lost components. Initiatives that have reintroduced the Southern Flying Squirrel to the Park, relocated administrative and maintenance facilities outside Park boundaries and restored specific sites within the Park, for example, have all contributed greatly to the improvement of the integrity of the Point Pelee ecosystem.

Summer in Canada's Deep South

Summer, leisure and Point Pelee go hand in hand. For more than a century, the Point has been a beloved escape from the stifling heat and humidity of an Essex County summer. Still today the single most popular activity in the Park is "beaching" – swimming, sunbathing and picnicking – along the Point's 20 kilometres (12 miles) of sandy shoreline. Point Pelee boasts the longest continuous natural beach in Essex County.

But summer is also a time for many other activities at the Park. Something as simple as a drive through the Park can provide many memorable surprises, like the sight of deer, standing peacefully by the road. In some wooded areas, where the trees form a natural canopy overhead, shafts of sunlight pierce the ceiling of this natural tunnel, highlighting the forest floor in the early morning mist. Wildflowers bask in the light afforded them along the road, paving it in an avenue of colour.

For those wanting something more active, the Marsh Boardwalk, the DeLaurier History Trail, or a hike to the tip are popular reasons for getting outdoors. Walking, another of the Park's most popular activities, is enjoyed by way of more than 12 kilometres of Park trails. Themed trails such as the DeLaurier House and Trail and the Woodland Nature Trail invite visitors through an excursion of cedar savannah, dryland and swamp forest.

Two-thirds of the Park is composed of freshwater marshes. This marsh is, in fact, one of the largest on all of Lake Erie. The marsh is a smorgasbord of sight, sound and colour: the wind through the lush, green cattails; pristine, white Water Lilies; vibrant, yellow Spatterdock; shocking-pink Rose Mallow; a frog hanging in the black water, as if suspended in space; a basking turtle; raucous,

" Every day we'd walk on the beach, play in the woods, go out on the fishing boats. We had no radios. We had oil lamps. The parents played cards by oil lamp at night all the time. And you knew who was French because they slammed their cards down on the table (laughter). It didn't take anything to amuse us. "

Joan Cross Date of Birth May 1, 1922. A Park camper in the summers of 1930 to 1934.

than 100 species a day is the rule, rather than the exception, for experienced birders.

The month of May at the Park is a bustle of human activity. Birdwatchers descend on the Park in droves. Despite the best intentions of the bird enthusiasts, this concentrated level of visitation can impact the vegetation and disrupt wildlife. But, care and consideration can minimize the amount of environmental impact that so many people, over a short period of time, can cause in such a small, fragile area. Park staff are reducing the impact on the environment by limiting the number of trails into prime birding areas and by actively promoting "Operation Spreadout," a program to inform birders of other birding "hotspots" in the area. Administrators hope that dispersal of birders among these other sites for part of their stay will help reduce some of the "crush" on the Point.

swooping terns, and solitude. While the marsh boardwalk offers an exceptional view of this environment, the best way to explore beyond the boundaries of the boardwalk and into the peaceful mysteries of the marsh is by canoe or kayak. These experiences provide the occasion to see the marsh as the natives and early European explorers did hundreds of years ago. Adventurers have an opportunity to gain an appreciation of this habitat

as they glide through this seemingly uncharted world.

Biking is another popular activity in the Park. In 1985, the Canadian Parks Service joined with Tourism Canada and the Friends of Point Pelee to rejuvenate Point Pelee's biking trail. Known now as the Centennial Trail, it provides bikers with a safe link, free from automobile traffic, between the Marsh Boardwalk and the Visitor Centre. Along its

For generations, the summer pilgrimage to Camp Henry represented a rite of passage for area Boy Scouts. The two-acre property in the Park was first used by Scout Troops for camping in 1932 on the invitation of its owners Joseph Mount Henry and his wife Mary. Ownership was passed to Henry Community Camp, Inc., a non-profit corporation, in 1940 and then on to Boy Scouts of Canada in 1981 for a price of $60,000. That same year Parks Canada assumed ownership of the property for $61,000 with a 20-year lease back to the Boy Scouts. In 1998, the Camp Henry site was forced to close due to the presence of agricultural pesticides – used in the neighbouring apple orchard – in the Camp's soil. In 1999, Camp Henry was relocated to a campsite north of the Visitor Centre, ensuring that its storied tradition would survive for future generations of campers.

Source: Eugene Barna

4.5 kilometres (three miles), it passes through some of the most delightfully scenic and serene areas in the Park. Once at the Visitor Centre, bikers may continue to the tip along the main west road. During the peak season, this is the road that is used by the transit system, so it too is free of most traffic.

A Pelee Fall

Few sights delight and stir the curiosity of the fall visitor to Point Pelee more than the butterfly tree. An annual event, it is produced by hundreds of roosting Monarchs. It delights by its sheer beauty. In late August, cool weather drives the Ontario Monarch population south. Normally they begin to funnel into Point Pelee in early September. In a typical year, there is usually more than one peak, depending on weather conditions and on the density of the population for that particular year. The Monarchs gather at the Point's tip, awaiting favourable winds to carry them across the lake. In the evening, they clump together in the southernmost trees and shrubs. Temperatures below seven degrees Celsius (45 degrees Fahrenheit) will keep them there until morning, creating a spectacular show for the early visitor.

The sight of hundreds of Monarchs flexing their wings to catch the first warming rays of the rising sun is a scene well worth the early hour. They will not remain long. If conditions are right, all too soon the Monarchs will respond to the warming air, fluttering aloft, out over the lake and on to Mexico.

Although birders tend to concentrate on spring, the fall migration can be just as exciting. In the spring, migrants are in a hurry to get down to the serious business of raising young. Although the whole migration takes place over five months, individual species usually pass through quickly.

The fall migration is much more leisurely, with individuals of many species gradually wandering through the Point over several months. On reaching the tip, many will carry on, crossing the lake without hesitation. It is not surprising to see even small migrants, such as the Ruby-throated Hummingbird, fearlessly darting off across the lake for Ohio. In this way they use the extension of the peninsula to cross Lake Erie at its narrowest point.

Other species are reluctant to follow. Instead, they will mill around the tip in confused flocks, eventually retreating back up the Point. Among the more noticeable representatives of this group are the Blue Jays. Blue Jays are "water shy," and

Motor boats are no longer permitted in the Marsh except for research or rescue operations.

67

generally will not cross the lake. Instead, upon reaching the tip, they will retreat back along the Point. Flocks of nervous Blue Jays noisily rush up and down the Point, trying to avoid becoming a meal for one of the hundreds of migrating hawks swooping and soaring overhead, their "eagle eyes" searching the moving smorgasbord for a suitable meal. All of this action makes the Tip an exciting place to be in the fall, with the added bonus that it is one of the best sites in the Park to hawk watch.

Winter in the Banana Belt

Amusingly, Essex County has been called Canada's "banana belt." The label may have originated as an attempt to convince the country's neighbours to the south that "Canada's Deep South" doesn't experience the winter conditions that characterize Canada. Essex County does have its winter, but on the whole, it is shorter and milder than in most

skiing. Because of its flatness, the Park is especially good for beginners, while the more experienced skiers can really "get in the stride."

Skiing is not the only winter sport at Point Pelee. Skating on the marsh has always been popular, too. When conditions are safe, Park staff clear and surface an extensive area around the base of the main observation tower and along the south arm of the boardwalk. A drive through the Park, or a hike along the many trails can be enjoyed in any season.

Winter is the quiet time at the Park. The waves are frozen into stillness, and on a cold clear day after a snowstorm, the Park takes on an unbelievable serenity. Sometimes visitors can be lucky enough to see 12-metre high ice formations at the tip!

Completing the Visit

One of the best places to commence or complete the Point Pelee experience is the Visitor Centre. There, one can obtain information on a wide variety of topics. A large, colourful exhibit, employing photographic murals, audio-visual programs, models, dioramas, soft sculptures and a "hands-on" Discovery Room, encapsulates the Park's story. A 110-seat theatre offers more about Canada's National Parks system, and specific topics dealing with geology, history, and the fascinating life histories of some of the Park's inhabitants. Park Interpreters and the Friends of Point Pelee, a volunteer team of Park enthusiasts, are on-hand to help visitors better understand the language of nature, history and geology.

> 66 Mr. Moss always said that the postmaster's wages depended on how many stamps he sold, so he being a tobacco man in Leamington, he used to go down there and buy stamps from Clark to bolster Clark's sales up, you see. One day I was talking to Clark and said to him, 'well how are you doing Clark.' 'Oh' he said, 'awfully busy today... I'm registering a letter.' 99

Foster Jackson Park Enthusiast. Date of Birth 1892.

areas of Canada. Residents of Essex County can not count on snow each year; some years there is virtually none. However, when there is snow, Point Pelee can get more than its fair share, especially if the entire western basin of Lake Erie is frozen. Then, strong westerly storms drive any powdery snow that has collected on the frozen water inland, and the Point acts as a giant snow fence. These conditions produce the best cross-country

Middle Island

The colourful history of Middle Island spans a vast period of time with evidence of the earliest presence of lifeforms dating back to the Devonian period, well before the movement of glaciers eroded its hard rock.

Much more recently, it is likely that native peoples were hunting and camping in the vicinity of Middle Island approximately ten thousand years ago. With the arrival of Europeans in the western basin of Lake Erie more than three hundred and thirty years ago, the landscape of the various islands was to be altered quite rapidly. Middle Island was no exception.

Logging began in the late 1700s, with the removal of oak and cedar. After another century elapsed, passenger and commodity traffic had increased to such a degree that navigation aids were needed to ensure that vessels were protected from the countless reefs and small islands. The continuing occurrence of shipwrecks in the vicinity of Middle Island prompted the Department of Marine and Fisheries to authorize the construction of a lighthouse on Middle Island in the year 1871. One year later the lighthouse was operational. It remained lit until the sailing season of 1918.

From the middle of the 19th century until the first decades of the 1900s, the island was used by Pelee Islanders for grazing cattle and other domestic animals. During this era the first leisure use of the island began. A house was built to serve as a cottage during the summer season. Thereafter, the prohibition chapter of Middle Island's history commences.

From 1920 until December 5, 1933 Middle Island was a rip-roaring gambling centre. Games of chance and the sale of liquor became the occupations of this area. The island was owned by a Toledo man, who through sources known only to himself, let it be known that speed boat operators were available in the Port Clinton, Ohio, area for the 25 kilometre (15 mile) trip to Middle Island. A boat dock was extended to accommodate the volume of visitors. Middle Island became the watering hole and gambling place of America's Midwest and through word of mouth the message brought thousands of vacationers to Port Clinton as the jumping off place for a day, or days, of fun depending on each individual's capacity. Those who braved a race with the United States Coast Guard could purchase as much liquor as desired in hopes of smuggling it back into the country. Many tried: some failed, some succeeded.

In the interest of protecting its many rare and endangered plants and animals, the Nature Conservancy of Canada, along with Parks Canada and numerous private sponsors, purchased Middle Island, the most southern place in Canada, in 1999. Middle Island became part of Point Pelee National Park in 2000.

Stratified Middle Devonian Limestone.

Buster Williams became caretaker of Middle Island at the age of 25, in 1929. The FBI would show up from time to time. According to his daughter, on one such occasion Williams, upon returning from Pelee Island, was greeted by an agent toting a machine gun. With great confidence Williams instructed the man to use the gun, or put it down. The agent put the machine gun aside.

But the business of gangsters and opportunists would only last a brief time, ending by 1933. Once again the island became quieter, with only the occasional visitor coming to enjoy the hospitality of the clubhouse. As time passed the dramatic evidence of human occupation began to fade. Neglected lawns and runways were invaded by native plants; heron rookeries reappeared and other animals were given the freedom to return when the ice provided a bridge from islands to mainland.

Middle Island was bought back from the United States in 1999 to become part of Point Pelee National Park, and as such, will remain protected for future generations. No one lives on it. The old house that served as a hotel, restaurant, gambling casino and outlet for good liquor, still stands, almost in ruins. A small, equally run-down building is near by. There are some who still believe that vessels with drag nets could reap a harvest of bottles, bags and wooden cases of liquor that had to be thrown overboard when Coast Guard cutters came alongside for inspection.

Blind Pigs

Under the terms of the Ontario Temperance Act, Bill 100 of 1916, no establishment could stock or sell any beverage with an alcohol content above 2.5 percent. Previously, the alcohol content of beer had been nine percent. All bars, clubs and wholesale liquor outlets were banned. Under the new Act, a person could not have, keep, give or consume liquor except in a private dwelling. The Act did not prohibit the manufacture of liquor by licensed companies, nor did it prohibit the importation or exportation of liquor.

Canadian Rum Runner
A LEGEND TO ISLANDERS **by John Switzer**

In 1928 a rum runner named Max, out of Wheatley, Ontario, fell in love with Magi, a beautiful young maid at the hotel on South Bass Island. They met when Max was making deliveries to Speak Easies on the island. Max and his boat, the *Midnight Fox*, were legends on the lake. The Coast Guard badly wanted Max. The story goes that Max planned one last run before the busy July 4th weekend. Then he would return to Canada with Magi. Max made the delivery, and with Magi aboard, was just leaving the island when he encountered a 40-foot Coast Guard boat that had been waiting in ambush. The Coast Guard opened up with a hail of deadly machine gun fire, the story said. When, in the darkness, the guardsmen pulled closer they found only bits and pieces of the boat floating on the water. They thought it had sunk with all aboard. Over time, the story said, the islanders often thought of Max and Magi. Then in 1942, when World War II news filled everyone's thoughts, this personal notice appeared in the weekly daily news: "To my beloved Captain Max Fox of the Canadian Royal Navy, whose life was taken by a German torpedo in the North Atlantic. Please rest now, my warrior, may all your Midnights be filled with my love, Magi."

The Banner

Detroit Free Press, November 13, 1888

Now scattered along the beach near Fish Point [between Pelee Island and Middle Island], she came ashore late Thursday afternoon in the north east gale. It was soon evident that she had made her last trip, as great seas rolled over her. The captain had his wife on board and a crew of five sailors, and their position was perilous. Without knowing how soon the old boat would go to pieces they were driven to the rigging where the captain lashed his wife and then himself. Night came on, and with it the gale increased, but at last help came. A number of local seamen manned a yawl boat and heroically went to the rescue. After much difficulty all the people were taken off the wreck, which soon afterward began to break up. *The Banner* was owned by Captain Webb, of Mount Clemens, Michigan. It was valued at $2,500. She had a small cargo of lath and shingles. There was no insurance on the vessel or the cargo.

The Purple Gang

Canadian whiskey sales in 1920 was reported to be $219 million. More contraband liquor was carried over Lake Erie than over all the other Great Lakes combined. In Ontario in 1920 there were 29 breweries and six distilleries given approval to manufacture liquor.

The Purple Gang of Detroit engaged in booze shipment and bootlegging. The gang controlled many Detroit-area Speak Easies. The use of violence, more than astute business practice, accounted for their survival next to competitors. It is believed that the Purple Gang was connected to Middle Island during the prohibition era. Liquor and beer were exported from the island. The Purple Gang's influence declined in 1929 following inter-gang murders and the conviction of some of their notorious leaders.

Due South

Middle Island, Canada's southernmost soil, is located about four kilometres (2.4 miles) southwest of Pelee Island. One of the nine Canadian islands in the Lake Erie Archipelago, the 21-hectare island is situated only 100 metres (110 yards) from the Canada-United States border.

Most of the island is wooded, with Hackberry being the predominant species. Similar to Point Pelee and Pelee Island, Middle Island contains natural geological features, landforms, flora, fauna and a climate which are rare in Canada. The island also represents a site very near its natural state.

the entire right to the Island for five hundred dollars. In 1834 McCormick moved his entire family to the Island. As early as 1836, the three oldest McCormicks – Alexander, John and William – managed the sawmill, shipping cedar and oak timber to the United States and Europe for shipbuilding.

Dr. F. Burrell McCormick was the visionary behind the construction of the Island's first hotel, offering rooms to summer tourists and fishing parties. As a summer resort, Pelee Island had distinct advantages, being easily attainable from Ohio's populated north shore all the way to industrial Detroit. Pleasure seekers from Kentucky and New York also took in the enjoyment of summer recreation on the Island.

David McCormick opened the first mercantile business on Pelee Island and was part owner of the original trading post located on Fish Point. The Island was organized as a township in the winter of 1867 and its first reeve was Arthur McCormick. The population was about 300 of which 60 were school children. It contained two school houses, a town hall and an Anglican church and consisted of $50,000 of taxable property.

Smith, Williams, and Co., a company from Kentucky that purchased land on the Island and proceeded to plant a vineyard and erect a wine cellar, recognized how "admirably adapted the Island was for grape culture." The American entrepreneurs also noted with surprise the presence of fruit trees, peaches in particular, and revelled in the fact that "everything common to this latitude grows admirably, even cotton has ripened, and the finer

Thaddeus Smith
1827-1902

qualities of tobacco can be cultivated."

The McCormicks also sold land to Thaddeus Smith, independent of his Smith, Williams, and Co. partners. Subsequently, Smith would become the owner and operator of Vin Villa Vineyards. The industry of winemaking had come to Pelee Island.

More than a century and a half after the McCormicks took ownership of the Island, their name remains prominent on present-day Pelee Island. Members of the pioneering McCormick family still reside on the Island. The name is rich in history and tradition, deeply rooted in the rocky island.

Alvar-Estonian: a term referring to the habitat defined by shallow soil over limestone. It is characterized by high PH and drastic changes in moisture content (from arid to wet).

A Natural Paradise

Pelee Island is home to many rare species of plant and wildlife found nowhere else in Canada. Pelee Island and neighbouring Middle Island are the southernmost territories in Canada. Their geographical position slightly south of the 42nd parallel latitude, coupled with the moderating effect of the lake on seasonal temperatures, make these islands the warmest summer locales in Canada and the most suitable climate in Canada for certain species of butterflies, trees, flowers, birds and turtles. As a comparison, this region of Ontario experiences 195 frost-free days next to the 201 frost-free days in Victoria, British Columbia. This provides for some of the rarest natural habitats in Canada

The inability of cacti to survive sub-zero temperatures makes Canada a very unsuitable habitat for the desert plant. The Prickly Pear Cactus, however, has developed a "cold resistance" and can be found on Pelee Island and Point Pelee National Park. The Prickly Pear, Canada's largest cactus, is noted for its large, waxy, "roselike" flower which blooms in late June and early July.

where Honey Locust, Hop Trees, Prickly Pear Cactus and Sassafras thrive in this unique climate.

Despite being removed from mainland Canada, Pelee Island has not proven to be immune to some of its harmful trends. Since the 1940s, progressive urban development, particularly in southern Ontario, has seriously diminished or completely extricated some species of plants and animals. As a means to thwart such tragedies, certain areas in southern Ontario were selected by government as preservation lands. It was in the 1970s that this preservation effort first came to Pelee Island.

Between 1973 and 1980 over 250 acres were designated to become Lighthouse Point Nature Reserve, occupying the Island's northeast corner. At about the same time, over 350 acres were sectioned to form Fish Point Nature Reserve at the Island's southwest end. Subsequently, a number of naturalist organizations have purchased land on the Island to be utilized as nature reserves as well.

One of the most sought-after Island discoveries by nature enthusiasts is the Blue Racer snake – a rare sighting because of the snake's undemonstrative nature and its limited population (there are roughly only two to four hundred Blue Racers inhabiting the Island). Another rare serpent found on the Island is the Lake Erie Water Snake. This reptile is devoted to the Island's beaches and rocky shoreline and can most readily be enjoyed basking in the southern sun on rocks or low-level tree branches at the water's edge. Pelee Island and its surrounding islands are the only places the Lake Erie Water Snake can be found in the world. Somewhat more curious in nature than the Blue Racer, the Water Snake is sometimes experienced a little too closely for a swimmer's liking.

The Fox Snake is spotted less frequently and is one of the largest of the snakes found on the Island. It can grow to almost two metres in length and is strikingly beautiful with its yellow body accented by its reddish-brown triangle pattern. A unique trait of the Fox Snake is its ability to mimic a rattlesnake's signature defense mechanism when startled. Unlike the ever-feared rattlesnake, the Fox Snake is gentle and not venomous.

Although Pelee Island is a less popular bird-watching destination than Point Pelee National Park from the standpoint of numbers of visitors, it offers an equally exceptional opportunity to witness the spring and fall migrations. Waves of beautiful birds come to rest and feed on the Island after flying for hundreds of kilometres at a time. Far from an undiscovered haven for birding, the spring season on Pelee Island is characterized by flocks of intrepid binocular-wielding, raincoat-clad enthusiasts in search of species of all kinds.

The plant life and wildlife on Pelee Island is guaranteed to inspire and excite. From snakes and birds to frogs and flowers, Pelee Island is a natural paradise.

A Guiding Light

Weathered and worn, the Pelee Island Lighthouse has faithfully kept its post for more than eight score years. Although this sentinel's guiding light was extinguished in 1909, the limestone structure has all the while stood dutifully on the Island's northeast corner, taking consolation in its modern day role as an Island attraction.

Built in 1833, its first light shone one year later to aid passing ships through the treacherous Pelee Passage. Nearly two centuries later, this lighthouse came to life again when in 2000 its restoration was completed through the ambitious efforts of the Island community. The refurbished beacon symbolizes the Island's storied history, its romance and its beauty.

This distinguished landmark is the second oldest lighthouse on the Canadian side of Lake Erie. In its company, one senses the danger that confronted early mariners in the days before modern navigation.

The waters off the shoreline at Lighthouse Point are shallow. The slowly graduating depths were difficult for seafaring captains to judge and many men were lost in Pelee Island waters. The Island's reefs were quick to claim any ship that failed to navigate through the Pelee Passage. Human error, Mother Nature and misguided maps all took their turn in drawing these vessels onto the Island's nautical burial ground. The Lighthouse Keeper would not only man the lantern, but also lead the rescue crews when needed.

Since the 1800s some 275 ships have come to rest on the lake's floor off the shores of Pelee Island and Point Pelee. Only 50 of those sunken giants have been found and explored to date. Fifteen of those are marked with a buoy system for public exploration. The majority of the wrecks

The closest shipwreck to the Island is only 65 metres (200 feet) off the shore of the lighthouse and about five metres (15 feet) below the water's surface. The *America* was a wooden passenger steamer measuring about two hundred and forty feet in length and was on her way to Detroit on April 5th, 1854 when she hit bottom and slowly sank. The crew and captain abandoned the ship with no lives lost.

The cargo that went down with many of the ships included oak, walnut, grains, ore and coal. It is believed that much of the sunken cargo was salvaged, looted by treasure hunters, buried under the shifting sands or, in time, washed up on shore. Of course, even more devastating than lost cargo was the loss of life. It is not known how many lives were lost at sea but the heroic rescue missions sent out from the Island were recorded. The documents from the rescue efforts were filed on Parliament Hill in Ottawa, but were destroyed by fire many years ago.

Pelee Island and the Municipality of Leamington are dedicated to preserving the submerged marine culture that forms an array of artificial reefs. The ships now provide an attractive habitat for fish and other underwater life. Increased visibility allows divers to explore the wrecks more extensively now. In the past, murky water hampered exploration efforts but over the past ten years the work of zebra mussels – introduced into the Great Lakes from ocean-going freighters – has increased visibility from ten to 40 feet. The Pelee Island Heritage Centre offers an informative and fascinating "on land" experience for shipwreck enthusiasts, as does the Marine Heritage Interpretive Centre on the mainland in Leamington.

have settled about 12 metres (40 feet) below the water's surface. The deepest ship rests almost 23 metres (74 feet) below the surface. The largest vessel to go down was named *CASE*. She was a wooden steamer built in 1889 and found her fate in 1917. The *CASE* was 301 feet long by almost 43 feet wide and for obvious reasons is the most popular dive site to date.

The Ironclad by Mary Mark

The Ironclad of Pelee Island is still a name that stirs the imagination of the Island's younger generation and arouses nostalgic memories among the older residents who remember the small craft which wrote an epic chapter in their Island's colourful history.

The Ironclad made its last run in the winter of 1927. To many in Canada's southernmost inhabited territory, it will be forever symbolic of the slogan "the mail must go through" as for years it was the only dependable link with the mainland from freeze up to break up. Long before the use of aircraft on Pelee Island, when navigation on Lake Erie closed in December, the Island was isolated. In severe winters, when ice conditions were good, teams of horses and sleighs could be used for the crossing. But this method was uncertain.

The Ironclad was a flat bottomed row boat very similar to a Cape Cod dory, and it had some of its sterling qualities, one of which was its adaptability. It was sixteen feet long with a beam of four feet. Galvanized iron sheathed the bottom and sides up to the gunwale to resist water and ice conditions. Underneath was a pair of oak runners, ironed off. The boat was fitted with a sail and boom which, when there was a favourable wind, aided travel immeasurably either on open water or on smooth ice.

The Ironclad carried mail, express, freight and even an occasional passenger twice a week, holding to a remarkably regular winter mail service between Island and mainland. Weather conditions had to be impossible to wash out the trip. This type of mail service began in 1879.

Ironclad, 1920s (mail service began in 1879)

93

The M.V. JIIMAAN has a passenger capacity of 400, a vehicle capacity of 34 and calls on the ports of Leamington, Kingsville and Pelee Island.

Coming Ashore

To reside on Pelee Island, permanently or seasonally, is to respect the fickle temperament of the lake that envelops you. Lake Erie can be most inviting, when placid or playful. But with little warning, the shallow lake can be worked up into a tumultuous fury. When the lake begins to rebel, Islanders take notice, especially when crops or produce are destined for mainland markets.

Many of the first docks built around the Island were constructed with shipping of Island products as their primary purpose. As the demand for Pelee Island's agricultural harvests increased, so did the demand for a more stable, functional dock on the Island's north end. Keeping up with the ever-changing market off the Island required agricultur-

al practices on the Island to evolve at the same pace. The importance of transportation of the Island's fresh harvest remained key to its survival as a significant provider of marketable goods.

As the tobacco era began to dwindle in the early 1930s, the Island farmers introduced the soya bean. Horses and threshing machines were used to harvest the new crops and the grain was shipped in bags by boat and then on by train or truck to the market. This process was expensive and tedious. In response, the federal government extended the Scudder Dock on the Island's north end. A grain elevator was erected on the dock allowing freighters in to load the grain in bulk. The building was completed in 1935.

The M.V. PELEE ISLANDER has a passenger capacity of 196, a vehicle capacity of 10 and calls on the ports of Leamington, Kingsville, Pelee Island and Sandusky, Ohio.

The first west side dock, Stone Dock, was built in the 1870s. A second dock was built on the Island's same side by Robert Little sometime around 1886. A third west side dock was built in 1901 which represented the Island's first Government Dock (West Dock). It was constructed from stone from the Island's own quarry. (The Pelee Island quarry was also a limestone source for the construction of the Niagara peninsula's Welland Canal and the City of Toronto's sidewalks.)

The logs that were used to support the dock were harvested on the Island's south end, hauled to the beach at Fish Point and then floated to the dock site.

In the early 1990s, the West Dock underwent a complete reconstruction to meet the strenuous agricultural and tourism demands of a changing island. The new landing welcomed the M.V. Jiimaan, a new 400-passenger ferry that together with the M.V. Pelee Islander, offers ferry service from Leamington and Kingsville and Sandusky, Ohio during the spring, summer and fall months.

Foreground: A.M. McCormick Grocery Store, built 1879.

A Doctor's Calling
Amherstburg Echo, March 2, 1888

Dr. S.A. King was suddenly called to Pelee Island on Monday evening of last week. The bad state of the rain made the crossing quite dangerous and it required more nerve than ordinary doctors possess to cross Lake Erie at this time of the year; but more is expected of the doctor than most men. As with all of his other accomplishments, he is a soldier and would cross Lake Erie on a cake of ice ten feet square if duty called, with nothing but his medical reputation for a paddle.

Dr. Townsend *(below)* lived on North Bass Island in the 1880s and served the adjacent islands as physician. He was known to cross the ice in the winter season with the aid of planks when a patient elsewhere was in need.

Vin Villa Press

Pelee Island Winery Label. Inspired by the unique nature that is Pelee Island, the Pelee Island Winery has always sought to capture the elements that make its viticultural area so special. Contemporary labels predominantly feature the local flora and fauna distinct to the Island's Carolinian habitat.

Island Vineyards

In 1891, Captain J.S. Hamilton, the president of Pelee Island Wine Company and J.S. Hamilton & Co., began construction of a three-story building with the stone being quarried from the Island. Named the Wine House, it was situated on five acres of land located near the West dock. The press was housed on the third floor, and the juice was channeled to the five thousand litre oak casks in the cellar. With Vin Villa Vineyards already well established, the new century began with a strong winemaking spirit on Pelee Island.

Seeking a longer growing season, the wine industry migrated from southern Ohio to the Lake Erie islands in the 1840s. The first vineyard on Pelee Island was planted in 1854 by Henry Price.

The first commercial planting and winery, Vin Villa, was the work of Thaddeus Smith and brothers D.J. and Thomas Williams in 1865. Life was still unsettled in the U.S. after the end of the war. This prompted the enterprising threesome to venture out of Kentucky, looking north for land opportunities. Soon after purchasing property at the north end of the Island – Sheridan Point – from the McCormick family, the business of winemaking began with twenty-five acres of grapes. Not long after the winery was complete, outbuildings and a cottage were built around the picturesque property, making the Vin Villa property one of the most breathtaking and prestigious properties on Pelee Island.

Five additional wineries were subsequently built on the Island, including that of J.S. Hamilton. The Wardropers joined the Smith family as pioneers in growing grapes on Pelee Island. Edward Wardroper and his brother John came from the United States as well. Born Englishmen from Sussex, they were raised in Alabama. In 1866 the brothers purchased land on the west shore of the Island and planted fifteen acres of grapes. Years later, in 1882, a wine cellar and house were built.

The Wardropers enjoyed a fertile career in winemaking. In 1897, at the peak of their company's success, The West View Vineyards transported sixty barrels of wine to Montreal by steamboat. One of the Wardropers' nephews, who lived on the Island with the winemakers, married Thaddeus Smith's daughter Minnie, bringing the two families even closer.

From the outset, Thaddeus Smith grew grapes for the sole purpose of making wine. By 1871, the first vintage was sold to wine manufacturers in Sandusky, Ohio. It was evident to him that this could be a flourishing industry. Smith aspired to sell his wine worldwide. He wanted to go it alone, buying the Williams brothers' shares and commissioning a fellow Islander to travel to the mainland to market the Vin Villa vintage. But it proved to be a fruitless adventure as the expenses incurred by the wine seller were barely being met by sales. A proud and determined man, Smith knew he had a good thing growing and would not be discouraged. Now selling the wine himself, his efforts took him to Brantford, Ontario, where he met with J.S. Hamilton, an established winemaker. Hamilton sampled the Vin Villa vintage and the relationship was sealed. He bought Vin Villa's entire stock. And so began the long and prosperous association between the two men.

Soon after Hamilton's introduction to Pelee Island, the wine was being sold all over the world.

Business was so good, Hamilton foresaw that the harvest of all the Island's wineries combined would not be enough to serve the demand. Additional wine cellars and the west side Wine House were operational by 1891. By the end of that growing season, Pelee Vineyards had record volumes of grapes for pressing. Long lines of horse-drawn wagons overflowing with grapes followed each other to the new wine house. If not for the J.S. Hamilton Wine House, the majority of the harvest may have soured on the vines.

The Vin Villa Vineyards continued its success until about the beginning of World War I. The next generation of Smiths found it increasingly difficult to keep their father's dreams alive year after year. Operating as a seasonal boarding house during the summer months, Vin Villa left the hands of the original family in 1923 in its sale to a Leamington doctor. The doctor restored the original property, replanted the vineyard and began making wine again. After a number of years, tending the large property and vineyard became too much of a chore for the doctor and the estate was rented in 1939 to John Hartman, one of his employees. Hartman too wished to keep the dream alive and continued the tradition of winemaking; however, only friends and family enjoyed the vintages.

Nine years after Hartman acquired the Vin Villa property, it was relinquished again, this time sold to the Feltz family who forewent the vineyards and raised livestock instead. The Feltz family is believed to be the last residents of Vin Villa before it was abandoned. Vin Villa's ultimate fate was determined in 1963 when it was destroyed by fire.

More than one hundred years after the first pioneer laid eyes on the Vin Villa property, the old winery ruins remain standing. The roots of its traditions are dug deep into the island's rock and in the minds of many Island residents. The historic

J.S. Hamilton & Co. winemakers.

establishment has lingered for decades, for years as a call to modern-day winemakers to return and prosper. The call was heard by wine manufacturers from distant lands in the late 1970s. Vineyards were reestablished on the Island by vintners from the winemaking regions of Austria and Germany. The Pelee Island Winery was erected on the mainland in Kingsville for convenience of location. In the early 1990s, the Pelee Island Winery Pavilion was constructed on home soil, continuing the Vin Villa tradition of offering Island visitors and residents alike, a charming and spirited sanctuary for sampling and socializing.

History is predominant when speaking of the Pelee Island Winery and its vineyards. The tradition of winning awards for its wines, nationally

low soils consist of glacial deposits over calcium-laden limestone bedrock. Water levels are controllable due in large part to the Island's dyke system and pumping stations. Sun, soil and climate (and latitude) combine to create the ideal grape growing conditions. This microclimate, along with quality grapes, helps to produce the wines for which Pelee Island Winery has become famous.

The vineyards, comprised of European varieties of Vitis vinifera, represent the most important component of the winemaking process. Highly skilled viticulturists take meticulous care of the grapes during their maturation ensuring that they reach their full potential by harvest time. Today, Pelee Island wine is known and admired all over the world. Winery viticulturalist Bruno Friesen is passionate about its wine. Friesen maintains that the Island's unique weather conditions and soil types make wine produced from Pelee Island grapes, one of a kind. He often thinks of the pioneers in the 1890s and how they recognized the Island's unique niche in the wine market. He speculates that if it were not for the crash in prices that toppled the local industry, Pelee Island would be littered with wineries today. Friesen doesn't frown at the idea of other wineries coming to the Island, insisting that the stronger Pelee Island becomes in the grape growing industry, the better the rewards for the industry and the Island community itself.

The Winery and its Island Pavilion now welcome up to thirty thousand visitors each summer season, an assured testament to the reputation of its wines. Notwithstanding, as the fruits of its labour realize unprecedented notoriety, the Pelee Island Winery is ever mindful of its winemaking traditions on Pelee Island – achievements which began in isolation, on an island with two steamboat arrivals a week and without a post office or telegraph cable. And so, success is certainly savoured.

and internationally, began with a medal in 1878 in Paris. Pelee Island Winery is Canada's largest estate winery. With approximately 500 acres of vineyards on the Island, Pelee Island Winery is the only winery in Canada that has earnestly created an operation that is both a grape grower and winery. The context in which today's winery thrives is no different than that enjoyed by its 19th century forefathers. Due to the lake's effect, Pelee Island is afforded Ontario's longest growing season. Its shal-

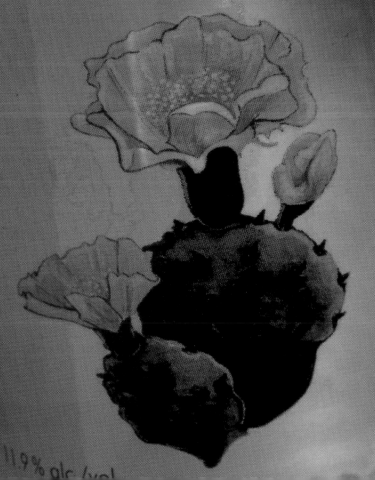

PELEE ISLAND WINERY

2001
Gewürztraminer
VQA Ontario VQA

750 ml

11.9 % alc./vol.

2000
Merlot
VQA Ontario VQA

Vin Rouge
750 m

Red Wine
13.2%

Product of Canada / Produit du Canada

Hulda's Rock

What would any island be without its own tale of unrequited love? This is a legend passed down by several generations of Aboriginal tradition. It is a story of star-crossed lovers and their tragic romance.

It is believed to begin when native peoples from the west abducted a French Canadian woman from Montreal. It was not uncommon in the early days of French occupancy of Canada for Aboriginal chiefs to make voyages to Montreal for trade or pleasure. It was also quite common for the native tribes to take white captives who were of good birth and education. This particular chief wanted a more secure place to hide his prize so he brought her to Pelee Island.

She was treated kindly and adopted by the tribe and eventually realized there was no escape off the Island. The unrelenting pleas of marriage from the young chief finally wore the captive woman down and she eventually married her captor.

Some years later, the couple had a baby girl, Hulda. The young maiden grew up with such beauty and grace that she attracted much attention. Her mother was determined to teach her daughter to speak, read and write French, her native language. Hulda was only 17 or 18 years old when a young Englishman came to the Island in search of adventure. He met Hulda and was enamoured by this promising woman and lingered on the Island longer than he had intended. The romance between the two blossomed and marriage

The following poem of Hulda's story was written by Bertha Smith, daughter of the original owner of Vin Villa Estates. She wrote it while attending boarding school on the mainland and once again brought this fabulous Island parable to life.

Once there lived on Point au Pelee
An Indian maiden blythe and gay,
Who often from her birch canoe
Would spear the spotted salmon through.

Pride of her Chieftain father's heart,
She oft would through the wild woods dart,
And with her bow and arrow raised
Would pierce the deer that calmly grazed.

Joy of her mother's loving eyes
This dusky maid was a household prize,
Whose beauty, grace and gentle arts
Won her a place in manly hearts.

A pale face to the Island came
To catch the fish and kill the game,
And when this lovely maid he knew,
She won his heart – she loved him too.

"Be mine, dear maiden," then he cried,
"Let me but win thee for my bride,
And on this Isle I'll gladly stay" –
The maiden did not say him nay.

Happy they lived from year to year,
Then tiding came of a mother dear,
Who dying, lay on a distant shore
And longed to see her son once more.

Then with the pledge to come again
Before another moon should wane,

The pale face parted from his bride
And o'er the waves his oars he plied.

But many moons did wax and wane,
The young wife's heart grew sick with pain,
And all her life grew dark and chill –
Her recreant husband tarried still.

At length a boat approached the shore,
Her heart beat high with hope once more –
But ah! For her that small white yawl
Bore a brief letter – that was all.

A letter that brought a withering blight
And broke a faithful heart that night;
That told a tale of broken trust
And hurled bright hopes down in the dust.

Hark! Hark, a wail of dark despair
Floats out upon the midnight air;
A splash is heard, and Pelee's pride
Floats out upon blue Erie's tide.

Upon the north of Pelee Isle,
There stranger linger but awhile;
View "Hulda's rock" – the mariner's guide,
That marks the fate of the Indian bride.

It marks that death-leap into the sea,
And marks a white man's perfidy.
The waves that 'gainst it foam and surge
Seem chanting e'er a funeral dirge.

ensued. The couple was living happily until word came that the Englishman's mother lay dying. He immediately departed for Montreal promising his young wife a quick return.

Many moons passed before Hulda received a letter telling a tale of broken trust. In complete despair, Hulda climbed to the top of a rock and leapt to her death in the waters of Lake Erie. The rock now symbolizes the meeting of two opposing cultures and the tragic end of a young woman. Hulda's Rock is still visible off the shore of the property occupied by the Vin Villa ruins. Myth has it that on a windy night the waves crash against her permanent gravestone chanting her name forever.

Tobacco workers pausing to pose in their fields.

Tobacco Industry

After the wine industry began on Pelee Island, other farmers were drawn to the island in search of additional sources of income. The tobacco industry was already firmly planted and beginning to flourish in other parts of Ontario. Tobacco, in a limited capacity, was already being grown on the Island, since the 1830s in fact. But it wasn't until the late 1890s that tobacco fields started to replace the vineyards.

The soil in the marshy areas of the Island proved to be perfect growing conditions for tobacco cultivation. By 1904 tobacco prices had skyrocketed, sending tobacco farmers running for the fields to plant more crops. In 1898 about seventy acres of burley tobacco were planted. By 1918, it is believed that over 600 acres were planted on the Island. In the 1920s, approximately one and a half million pounds of tobacco were harvested in a single season on Pelee Island. After the tobacco had been harvested it was "spudded" over a needle on tobacco sticks and then hung to cure in a ventilated barn. Once the leaves were cured they were stripped and packed in bales and shipped across the ice to the mainland by horse and sleigh.

The tobacco industry began to diminish in the 1930s leaving farmers searching for alternative crop solutions. At that time the soya bean was starting to play a significant role in the markets. And so it was that soya beans replaced much of the tobacco industry on Pelee Island.

The Big Marsh

The deep canals that course along many of the Island's roadways are in many respects the safeguard to the Island's existence. Both unassuming and daunting at the same time, these drainage veins preserve its way of life. The story of these waterways begins in 1878 with Lemeul Brown and his aspirations to drain the Island's marshes so that they could be farmed. Through Brown's chance meeting of Dr. John M. Scudder of Cincinnati, who had visited Holland and witnessed the Dutch reclamation works in the North Sea, the two men together set out to drain the water-inundated land.

By 1885 the duo had purchased the Big Marsh – over 4,000 acres at two dollars an acre – and had begun to build skows and dredges. The failure of their early trials led to an invitation to the Chatham Dredging Company to perform the digging. By 1886 a steam driven scoop-wheel, 28 feet in diameter, was in place at the north end of the Island. Twenty kilometres (12 miles) of canals were dug and water began to flow toward the north pumping station which then dumped it into the lake. The system quickly lowered marsh waters by 18 inches and merged three land masses.

A second pumping station was commissioned in 1892 to manage the quantity of water flowing through on a daily basis more efficiently. After strenuous efforts blasting bedrock, and repairing dredges and dykes, the West Shore Road pumping station was complete, improving upon the operations of the original station. The pumps were to move sixteen hundred gallons of water per minute. The metal building that stands today replaced the original cedar structure after it was destroyed by fire in 1939. While the system's purpose has remained unchanged, diesel motors have replaced the boilers and paddle wheels.

The drainage of the marshes displaced wetland amphibians, birds and plants, while bringing an influx of human settlers lured by thousands of acres of very fertile virgin farmland. And so agriculture progressed on Pelee Island.

God's Acre

In the 1890s, the Islanders had to do the unimaginable. They were faced with the challenge of moving the Island cemetery to a safer site. Located on the shore of Sheridan Point just south of the Pelee Club, the original ossuary was washing away from erosion. To ensure an eternal resting place for lost loved ones, the graveyard was moved to its current location, an inland haven on what is now called Cemetery Road. A visit to the cemetery approaches a step back in time, with its seclusion interrupted only by the trickle of light through its densely-treed surroundings.

An informal visit to these grounds immerses any guest in the Island's rich human history. Aging tombstones and heart-felt scriptures captivate even the most casual visitors. A stroll around the *old* fraction of the cemetery is truly entrancing. Elderly trees tower protectively over the graves like an umbrella giving sanctuary to those beneath it. Weathered branches watch over the Island's most valuable asset – its ancestors.

Among many others, occupants of the cemetery include Island forefather William McCormick, who died in 1840, and Frederick Fisher, Chief of the Chippewa Nation. The Schulthies, the family who accompanied Thaddeus Smith to Pelee Island from Kentucky, are buried here as well. The entourage of German immigrants brought over by Lemuel Brown after he had reclaimed the Big Marsh is found throughout the graveyard.

The picturesque setting of the Pelee Island Cemetery invites the company of passersby, and asks strangers to meet its inhabitants and hear its story. One of the most poignant messages – a scripture on a tombstone – comes as a mother's last gift to her children in the form of reassurance that she is not dead, but just sleeping there.

111

Fishing Industry

Commercial fishing around Pelee Island has been successful since 1845, the year David McCormick and Henry Leighton established the first fishery on the Island. At that time pound nets were used in the waters around the Island. The nets forced fish to follow a long lead through a funnel into an end trap. This proved to be a lucrative way to catch the fish in mass quantities. In 1900 a fishing inspector's report indicated that the Island fishery har-vested a variety of different species including Lake Herring, Pike, Whitefish, Sturgeon, Pickerel (also known as Walleye), Perch and Catfish – as well as caviar – which were exported predominantly to the United States.

Today, one fishery is still in operation on Pelee Island. Harris Fishery catches mostly White Bass, Pickerel, Yellow Perch and White Perch and sells to both Canadian and American companies.

Members Only

The sign reads "Private Property Keep Out". But as the last tributary feeding off an inconspicuous dusty dead end, this quiet laneway readily tempts even the most conscientious Island visitor. Its sole destination may be the most distinguished and enigmatic property on the Island today by way of its storied guest list. Perched above a rocky shoreline, the Pelee Club stares out at Lake Erie's western basin from the Island's northwest corner.

The Pelee Club, a "members only" facility, cele-

brated its grand opening in October, 1883. Its exclusive amenities included gas lighting, running water, billiards and a bowling alley. The Pelee Club prided itself on its privileged membership. Initially the Club welcomed only 25 members, a number that eventually grew to 50. Among the most influential to pass through the Pelee Club were U.S. Presidents Grover Cleveland, Rutherford Hayes and William Howard Taft.

The Pelee Club was established by a small group of avid American fishermen. The fishing group usually slept in tents during their excursions but one night a fierce storm drove them to the doorstep of neighbouring Vin Villa seeking shelter. The men revelled in the luxury of Vin Villa and elected to board there for a number of years thereafter. They yearned for an Island facility of their own. Eventually, they bought property from Thomas McCormick for $800 and built their clubhouse on the north tip of the Island.

Over one hundred years after this private club was forged, it still exudes a mysterious and reticent personality. The current owners remain committed to its reclusion and tradition. The Pelee Club today still operates with its original purpose unchanged. But with permission, a visitor to the Island may be treated to a peek into the old bowling alley and an aura of a different time. The original bowling balls still lurk about. Old gas lamps cling to the walls. The smell of old pipe smoke still lingers in the air. The once pristine wood floors are now slanted from the weight of time. And the banter of distinguished guests of yesteryear still echoes from room to room, if one can imagine it.

Southern Hospitality

Time on Pelee Island renders an appreciation of the many anecdotes that most of its antiquated buildings, ruins and empty meadows have to offer. The old Gillis Lodge is no exception.

Around 1883, American merchants from Ohio owned almost one hundred acres across from the schoolhouse on Stone Road. There they built four buildings including the house later to be known as Gillis Lodge. Tenant farmer John Jupp lived on the land until 1905 when he decided to move his farm: the old house as well. The Jupp family continued to live in the uprooted house until the 1920s. A second house was moved onto the property. The Jupps had the two houses renovated into one large building.

It is not clear how long the Jupp family owned and tended the land on Mill Point but sometime during the 1920s, the lodge is believed to have housed Al Capone during prohibition. As the legend goes, Capone used the Island as a safe haven to move booze during the bootlegging era. However, Capone and his associates were not in the habit of leaving evidence of their presence behind, and as such there isn't anything hard and fast to corroborate the story. Tale has it that there are still bottles of alcohol hidden within the walls of the old Gillis Lodge.

John L. Lidwell is thought to have lived in Gillis Lodge sometime in the mid-1930s and until the late 1950s operated the facility as a fishing and hunting lodge for seasonal guests. In 1985, after sitting abandoned for nearly 30 years, the neglected Gillis Lodge was refurbished and reopened. Under new ownership and a new name, Mill Point Lodge became one of the Island's first bed and breakfast establishments. Annually, it opened its doors in early spring to accommodate bird watch-

The Tin Goose Inn at Mill Point, the southeast corner of Pelee Island.

ers, welcomed summer tourists and travellers from far and wide and closed for the winter season only after seeing off the last pheasant hunter in November.

In the mid 1990s the Lodge exchanged hands again. A new vision for its appearance and level of service married long-standing tradition with modern-day trends. Today, operating as the Tin Goose Inn, guests and passersby alike marvel at the brilliant charm of the salient old building and its inviting property.

The Pheasant Hunt

The Annual Pheasant Hunt of 2002 marked seventy years of continued tradition on Pelee Island, a particularly prosperous economic endeavour for the Island community.

In 1968, the Island's Pheasant Farm was established to raise pheasant chicks to stock the Island's natural habitat for hunt time. More than twenty thousand birds are raised and released for three consecutive fall hunts and the winter hunt.

It all began in 1880, when the Ring-necked Pheasant was introduced to the United States from China. Seventeen years later, four pairs of pheasants were brought to Pelee Island but the mating process turned out to be tedious. It wasn't until 1918, when two crates of pheasants from Ohio were brought to the Island, that the population began to grow and flourish. The birds quickly became a nuisance to local farmers who were forced to approach Town Council about a solution to their damaged crops.

In 1932, the first pheasant hunt was organized. Twenty-one hunters gathered for the two-day hunt in late October. But as the popularity of the hunt waxed, the pheasant population waned. It's

believed that over the years, an increase in predators was contributing to the game bird's diminishing numbers. The hunters were left without prey and the Island without a valuable commodity. Eventually it was decided that the raising of birds to meet the demands of the hunt was the answer.

Pheasant Hunt: *(left to right)* Bruce Webster (holds record for participating in 59 consecutive Hunts), Bill Hines and Bob Clark.

Formerly the South-end School House, the building is now used as a privately-owned cottage.

School Days

The first young students on Pelee Island were likely tutored and then sent off the Island for higher education. But in 1870, a public school board was elected and two schoolhouses were built on the Island. In 1880 both schools were closed permanently due to a smallpox outbreak, but one year later four more schoolhouses were built and by 1900 there were about 285 children attending the four schools. The South-end School on Stone Road was destroyed by fire in 1913 but rebuilt without delay and still stands today.

The brick schoolhouse that is presently used was one of the four additional schools built on the Island in 1917. With just three rooms, the students learn alongside other children of various grade levels. Upon graduation from Pelee Island's elementary school, students move their studies to the mainland, obtaining their secondary education in Kingsville. The teens board with families during the school week, only returning home to the Island on weekends and for the summer.

Tale of the Lake Erie Monster

Islanders won't speak about it publicly, but word has it that some have seen it. It has been said that an ancient creature lurks beneath the surface of the deeper, colder fresh waters of Lake Erie.

The snake-like lake monster is said to be about twelve feet long and a few feet wide with an eel's head that protrudes above the water's surface. The first sighting of this monster fish was recorded in the *Amherstburg Echo* newspaper in the 1880s. The story told of a fisherman who arrived in Amherstburg's port shivering with fright. He described seeing a gigantic snake-like fish travelling quite quickly and leaving a wake with its head above water. An alleged sighting of similar description was recorded in the summer of 1998 just off the shores of Hen Island, a neighbouring island to Pelee in Lake Erie's Western Basin.

Opposite: Lake Henry, located at the northeast corner of the Island.

photography index

sponsor index

Century 21 Erie Shores Realty Inc.
(An Air Miles Reward Office)

106 Talbot St. East
Leamington, Ontario N8H 1L5
tel: (519) 326-8661
fax: (519) 326-7774
email: c21leam@c21erieshores.com
website: www.c21erieshores.com

14 Main St. West
Kingsville, Ontario N9Y 1H1
tel: (519) 733-8411
fax: (519) 733-6870
email: c21king@c21erieshores.com
website: www.c21erieshores.com

At Century 21 we maintain a highly trained staff of real estate professionals and we take great pride in relocating many clients to this vibrant region (Canada's South shore). Vic Tiessen (Sales Rep.) has been specializing in Pelee Island sales for over nine years. Give Vic or anyone of our professional sales staff a call today!

Comfort Inn Leamington

279 Erie Street South
Leamington, Ontario N8H 3C4
tel: (519) 326-9071
fax (519) 326-3445
website: www.choicehotels.ca/cn276

Corporation of the Municipality of Leamington, Economic Development Office

38 Erie St. North
Leamington, Ontario N8H 2Z3
tel: (519) 326-5761
fax: (519) 326-2481
email: info@townofleamington.ca
website: www.info@townofleamington.ca

The Municipality of Leamington. Friendly gateway to the natural wonders of Point Pelee National Park and Pelee Island. Explore one of the most diverse and unique eco-systems in Canada. Experience our southern Ontario hospitality. For tourist information contact: 1-800-250-3336. Visit our website at: www.townofleamington.ca. Send inquiries to: info@townofleamington.ca.

Essex Community Futures Development Corporation/ Société d'aide au développement des collectivités

33 Princess St., Suite 212
Leamington, Ontario N8H 5C5
tel: (519) 326-1863
fax: (519) 326-5521
email: info@essexcfdc.on.ca
website: www.essexcfdc.on.ca

The Essex CFDC/SADC is a non-profit federally funded organization established to help the rural community strengthen its local economy and create jobs. It does this by providing business-counselling

support, loans to small business, and by working closely with its community partners in supporting community economic development.

Family Tradition Foods Inc.

P.O. Box 869
R.R.#1 Drovers Road
Wheatley, Ontario N0P 2P0
tel: (519) 825-4673
fax: (519) 825-3134
website: www.familytradition.com

Cultivating great taste... We are grateful to all those "Islanders" who have helped make our annual Family Tradition "Snap Bean Trial" a success each year. We will continue to include Pelee Island as a destination point during our customers' visits.

Gulliver Insurance Brokers Ltd., a Hub International Company

33 Princess St., Suite 501
Leamington, Ontario N8H 5C5
tel: (519) 326-2689
fax: (519) 326-0128
email: mreidl@thehubgroup.com
website: www.hubinternational.com

Mennonite Savings and Credit Union

Leamington Branch
243 Erie St. South
Leamington, Ontario N8H 3C1
tel: (519) 326-8601 or (888) 285-5501
fax: (519) 326-4659
website: www.mscu.com

Owen Sound Transportation

343 - 8th St. East
Owen Sound, Ontario N4K 1L3
tel: (519) 376-8740
fax: (519) 376-6384

Pelee Island Winery

455 Seacliff Drive (County Road #20)
Kingsville, Ontario N9Y 2K5
tel: (519) 733-6551

toll-free: (800) 597-3533
fax: (519) 733-6553
email: pelee@peleeisland.com
website:
www.peleeisland.com

Pelee Island Winery is Canada's largest estate owned winery, with close to 600 acres of vineyards which produce mostly European vines including Chardonnay, Pinot Noir, Cabernet, and Merlot. Since 1985, Pelee Island Winery has focused on the "nature of the island" to develop its brand and reputation. Nearly every label developed has evolved around a characteristic unique to the island: the 1999 Cabernet Franc features the gray fox, the 2000 Gewurztraminer displays the prickly pear cactus and our popular 2000 Vidal hosts the distinctive Monarch butterfly. Since the creation of the VQA (Vintner's Quality Alliance) in 1989, Pelee Island Winery has become the #1 best seller of VQA red and white wines in Canada. For over 20 years, Winemaster and General Manager Walter Schmoranz has committed the winery to excellence through his integrity and passion for winemaking.

Sun-Brite Canning Ltd.

2526 Talbot Road
P.O. Box 70,
Ruthven, Ontario N0P 2G0
tel: (519) 326-9033
fax: (519) 326-8700
website: www.sun-brite.com
Sun-Brite Canning Limited was incorporated in 1973

to provide high quality canned tomato products to the food industry. Our attention to quality has not gone unnoticed. Sun-Brite has been awarded the coveted "Campbell's Select Supplier" honour and the "Supplier of the Year" by Little Caesars. Over the years, Sun-Brite has introduced pizza, spaghetti, all purpose sauces, tomato puree and a variety of packaged beans to its product line. In 1997 Sun-Brite acquired Unico Inc., a recognized brand name in the retail food industry. Today, Sun-Brite is still evolving.

Woodslee Credit Union

328 Main St. East, Kingsville
tel: (519) 733-5231
141 Erie St. South, Leamington
tel: (519) 326-8641
online banking: www.woodslee.com
telephone banking: (519) 776-4311
or toll free 1-800-492-9492

Woodslee Credit Union is a full service financial institution with additional branches in: Harrow, Amherstburg, Belle River, Essex, Woodslee and a sub-branch on Pelee Island. Founded in 1943 we will celebrate our 60th Anniversary in 2003.

www.pelee.com

400 - 601 W. Broadway
Vancouver, British Columbia V5Z 4C2
tel: (604) 871-4315
fax: (604) 871-4317
email: claudia@pelee.com
website: www.pelee.com

proceeds

Partial proceeds from the sale of each copy of *Pelee Portrait - Canada's Southern Treasures* will go to support initiatives of the *Friends of Point Pelee* and the *Pelee Island Heritage Centre*.

The Friends of Point Pelee

Established in 1981 as a cooperating association, the *Friends of Point Pelee*, through its member, volunteer and voluntary activities and contributions, and in partnership with Parks Canada, is dedicated to protecting and presenting a nationally significant example of Canada's natural heritage in Point Pelee National Park. The *Friends of Point Pelee* also endeavours to foster public understanding, appreciation and enjoyment in ways that ensure Point Pelee National Park's ecological and commemorative integrity for present and future generations.

The Friends of Point Pelee
1118 Point Pelee Drive
Leamington, Ontario N8H 3V4
tel: (519) 326-6173
email: fopp@wincom.net

Pelee Island Heritage Centre

The *Pelee Island Heritage Centre* was founded in 1988. Its mission is to research, preserve and interpret the rich diversity of the Island's human and natural heritage. The *Centre* has sponsored research, publications, summer education programs, and restoration of the local landscape. The Museum's collection is open daily from 10 a.m. to five p.m. from May 1st until November 1st. Publications, prints and videos are available for purchase at the *Centre*.

Pelee Island Heritage Centre
1073 West Shore Rd.
Pelee Island, Ontario N0R 1M0
tel: (519) 724-2291
email: pimuseum@mnsi.net